Testing Your Mettle

I've come to the frightening conclusion that I am the decisive element in the classroom. It's my personal approach that creates the climate. It's my daily mood that makes the weather. As a teacher, I possess a tremendous power to make a child's life miserable or joyous. I can be a tool of torture or an instrument of inspiration. I can humiliate or humor, hurt or heal. In all situations, it is my response that decides whether a crisis will be escalated or de-escalated and a child humanized or de-humanized.

—Haim Ginott

Testing Your Mettle

Tough Problems and Real-World Solutions for Middle and High School Teachers

Harry J. Alexandrowicz

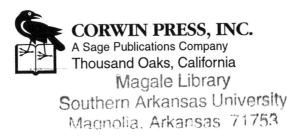

CORWIN PRESS, INC.
A Sage Publications Company
Thousand Oaks, California

For information:

Corwin Press, Inc.
A Sage Publications Company
2455 Teller Road
Thousand Oaks, California 91320
E-mail: order@corwinpress.com

Sage Publications Ltd.
6 Bonhill Street
London EC2A 4PU
United Kingdom

Sage Publications India Pvt. Ltd.
M-32 Market
Greater Kailash I
New Delhi 110 048 India

Printed in the United States of America

Library of Congress Cataloging-in-Publication Data

Alexandrowicz, Harry J.
    Testing your mettle: Tough problems and real-world solutions for
    middle and high school teachers / by Harry J. Alexandrowicz.
        p.   cm.
    Includes bibliographical reference.
    ISBN 0-7619-7752-X (cloth) — ISBN 0-7619-7753-8 (pbk.)
    1. Teacher effectiveness—Handbooks, manuals, etc.   2. School
    discipline—Handbooks, manuals, etc.   I. Title.
    LB1775 .A414 2001
    371.1'02'4—dc21   00-011238

01   02   03   04   05   06   07   7   6   5   4   3   2   1

Editorial Assistant:	Julia Parnell
Production Editor:	Diane S. Foster
Editorial Assistant:	Cindy Bear
Typesetter/Designer:	Lynn Miyata
Cover Designer:	Michael Dubowe

Contents

AUTHOR'S NOTE: This table of contents is organized by main topics. Since most actions in education do not happen in isolation, most snapshots are not limited to one topic. Please refer to "Cross-Reference of Topics and Snapshots" on p. ix to further investigate other topics.

Cross-Reference of Topics and Snapshots

Listed below are the various topics presented in the snapshots, along with references to the snapshot numbers as they appear in the body of the book.

Topic	Snapshot Numbers
Administrative relations	3-3
Authority of teachers and the school	1-1, 7-17
Cheating	3-1, 5-6
Child abuse	5-1, 5-2, 5-3, 5-4, 5-15
Choice of profession	7-1, 7-12
Civility in school	1-1, 1-2, 2-5, 2-11, 4-7, 6-4, 6-5
Classroom climate	1-1
Classroom management	1-3, 5-15
Confidentiality	7-2, 7-3, 7-13
Contractual obligation	7-12
Controversial topics	1-3
Crisis management	5-14, 7-9

Topic	Snapshot Number
Search and seizure	2-5, 2-8, 5-6, 5-7, 5-9, 5-11, 5-13
Sexual behavior	1-2, 2-1, 2-4, 2-5, 3-5, 5-1
Sexual conduct	2-10, 2-11
Staff impropriety	2-3, 3-4, 3-5, 5-10, 6-3
Student rights	1-1, 5-7
Substance abuse	2-7, 2-10, 4-5, 5-7, 5-8, 5-9, 5-10, 5-11, 5-12, 5-13, 6-2, 7-2, 7-16
Suicide threats	7-3
Teacher as public persona	3-2, 3-5, 4-2, 7-4, 7-14, 7-15, 7-16, 7-17
Teacher evaluation	3-3
Teacher misconduct	6-5
Teacher responsibility	2-4, 4-1, 5-8, 5-10, 5-12, 5-13, 6-4, 7-2, 7-7, 7-8, 7-9, 7-10, 7-11, 7-12, 7-13
Teaching style	4-8
Threats	1-2, 2-9, 5-1, 5-3, 7-8, 7-11
Tort liability	1-4, 5-14, 5-15, 7-9
Truancy	2-6, 2-7
Trust	2-3, 5-4, 5-6, 7-3
Unions	4-5
Violence in school	1-4, 5-2, 6-2, 7-11
Weapons	2-8, 2-9

Preface

This book is designed to ask the difficult questions that teachers face every day. It brings forward many topics not addressed elsewhere. However, these questions are on the minds of both prospective and practicing teachers, that is, of any teacher who wants to be effective.

As a teacher, what would you do if

1. The school's best athlete is failing your class?
2. A parent threatens you?
3. You discover students are hazing other students?
4. You are accused of holding a student too tightly during a school dance?
5. You innocently attend a party and find students drinking beer there?
6. You see a gun in a locker?

These are only a sampling of the many issues that this book covers. Please read on and discover the issues in education that test the mettle of those who experience this world every day. You will find many answers and many more questions as you experience the snapshots included herein. Enjoy and reflect—what would you do?

Acknowledgments

Many individuals have helped, encouraged, berated, and cajoled me to make this book a reality. My appreciation is extended to the following individuals: Meredith Alexandrowicz, who encouraged me and shared the many situations she experienced during her teaching (may she be the best secondary science teacher ever); and Dr. Harold Kurtz, my friend and buddy, who pointed out where I was lacking in content.

But most of all, I thank all my students and colleagues, whom I have come to know and respect through the years. Remember, once we fail to learn from one another, we must abandon ship, because no port will be worth finding.

The contributions of the following reviewers are also gratefully acknowledged:

John Davis
Assistant Professor, Teacher Education Department
California State University, Dominguez Hills
Carson, CA

Joe Corral
Teacher
Anne Arundel County Board of Education
Annapolis, MD

E. Ann Adams
Associate Director, Staff Development
Clinical Instructor, Graduate School of Education
University of Utah
Salt Lake City, UT

Judy Butler
Assistant Professor of Education
State University of West Georgia
Carrollton, GA

Janice Bibik
Associate Professor
University of Delaware
Newark, DE

Sylvia Burger
History and Science Department Head
Calvary Christian Middle School
Dumfries, VA

About the Author

Harry J. Alexandrowicz is currently Superintendent of Schools in Woodland Township, New Jersey. He has provided 28 years of service to the southern New Jersey area as a teacher of social studies, assistant principal, high school and middle school principal, and superintendent. He has also served as an adjunct professor of educational foundations at Rowan University and has made numerous staff-development presentations throughout New Jersey and Pennsylvania. Glassboro State College (now Rowan University), Villanova University, Rutgers University, and Temple University have provided his formal training.

Alexandrowicz's goal has always been to provide teachers with the best training, as a solid educational foundation. He has worked with student teachers and teachers in all phases of their careers in the public schools and in the university classroom.

Readers' experiences with this book are of great interest to Harry. Please e-mail your comments, insights, issues, stories, or experiences to him at drowicz@bellatlantic.net. Only through professional sharing will we find better ways to help children.

Introduction

What many teachers complain about most is the lack of reality training in their formal education. Typical classroom lectures and exercises do not prepare individuals for problems and situations that will present themselves in the schools. Teachers need to think and act beyond the theory presented in educational textbooks. And that is why I have written this book.

The following pages provide an intellectual minefield of problematic situations that teachers encounter. Whether you believe that teachers are born or made, whether teaching is an art or a science, teachers must prepare for the unanticipated events and situations that will inevitably occur.

These snapshots are to be considered seriously. They are based on actual events during my 28 years of experience as a teacher, assistant principal, principal, superintendent of schools, and parent. Each snapshot contains an underlying legal, philosophical, or common-sense lesson. The snapshots that constitute the substance of this book are all nonfiction; however, all names and locations have been changed.

I have grouped the snapshots into chapters that parallel the major problematic areas teachers face every day—from students' behavior in and out of their classrooms to interactions with administrators and parents, complying with school policy, and other issues not so easily classified.

Each snapshot is organized as follows: vignette, the topical problem areas into which it falls, possible solutions, space for you to write your proposed action or solution, what actually happened, and what should have happened—and why. The four possible solutions are the

result of my presenting each snapshot to different members of the educational community. What appears here is based on what various
teachers, administrators, professors, parents, school secretaries, aver-
age citizens, and college students have had to say about realities in
schools. Notice that each response is different. Also notice that many
are emotional reactions to the details of the snapshot. One goal of this
book is to allow you to experience these snapshots and learn to think
logically on your feet. If you can learn to remove the emotionality from
your reactions, you will probably make better decisions.

Space is provided for you, the reader, to write your immediate reaction to each snapshot. Take note of how your initial reaction may
change after you have discussed these snapshots. What actually happened in each snapshot follows.

As noted above, the last section of each snapshot provides the
reader with commentary about what should have happened and why.
This is not to say these are the only solutions for each situation. However, based on experience and research, a teacher will gain some insight
and a basis for making decisions on the spur of the moment. By thinking the issues through in advance and by experiencing them vicari-
ously through this book, the teacher will be better prepared to make
better decisions.

Different snapshots reflect positions not only of teachers but also of
assistant principals, principals, superintendents, and other stake-
holders in the educational community. Sometimes, to understand a
teacher's perspective, you need to place yourself in that person's shoes.
Be honest in your reactions, and you will learn a great deal about what
makes the teacher a successful professional.

It is imperative that teachers develop a working knowledge of the
school district policies under which they are working. Unfortunately,
these policies are generally part of the pieces of information thrown at a
teacher as part of an orientation program that is often short. Teachers
are advised to study these policies, because actions taken by the teacher
must conform to them, and because the teacher is responsible for
enforcing such policies beginning the very first day of school.

Educational leaders have a tremendous obligation to provide the
physical environment and mental environment in which students can
achieve success. The future of America depends on the ability of educational leaders to prepare young people to meet the challenges of the
future.

Leaders are not necessarily members of the board of education, administrators, or parents. The highly successful teacher understands the entire educational community and the roles played by each stakeholder. The highly successful teacher assumes the appropriate role and applies learned skills well beyond the classroom. The goal is to create the best educational product for the community and society in general.

What Is Quality Teaching?

This book will be more valuable to everyone if there is an understanding of, working knowledge of, and agreement with the following statements:

- Each individual student has the right to a free, appropriate, public education in an environment that is free from physical danger and mental distraction.

- Each individual student is entitled to receive a course of study that is tailored to his or her abilities.

- Each individual student is entitled to receive a course of study that provides the opportunity to achieve full personal potential.

- Education is a lifelong process of acquiring skills, knowledge, and experience.

- Each individual student must be motivated to feel self-esteem, seek knowledge and truth, and develop social consciousness.

- Each individual student has the right to seek self-actualization.

- Learning takes place in an environment where everyone involved in the teaching-learning process understands their roles and expectations.

- Effective teaching results from a combination of planned actions and reactions: Each lesson has a beginning, middle, and end that links previous knowledge to new information and is measurable.

- Quality teachers are professional educators who are willing and able to do the following:

  1. Show concern for students.
  2. Remain competent in their field or discipline.

3. Exhibit enthusiasm in the classroom.

4. Develop the art and technique of effective presentation.

5. Create a positive image as a role model for the student to observe and emulate.

6. Take pride in their physical appearance and their teaching station.

7. Accept new responsibilities and participate in extracurricular activities.

8. Communicate with all members of the educational community relating to the progress, or lack of progress, of each child.

Being in Charge of Your Classroom

1

"Then You Must Be One, Too"

Ms. Cartmen is supervising detention after school one day when she notices a badge on Kasey Krim that reads, "I'm OK, You're a Shithead." The pin is quite large and can be read from across the classroom. Several students are pointing at Kasey and laughing. Ms. Cartmen believes that they are waiting to see her reaction.

Main Topic

Civility in school

Subtopics

Authority of teachers and the school

Classroom climate

Dress code

Student rights

Possible Solutions

Ms. Cartmen should

1. Take the badge from Kasey immediately.

2. Wait until the end of the detention period to confront Kasey.

3. Quietly call the vice-principal, and ask her to report to the detention room.

4. Let Kasey wear the badge, but ask him not to wear it in school gain.

5

What Would You Do?

_____

_____

_____

_____

_____

What Really Happened

Ms. Cartmen took the badge from Kasey immediately and took it to the principal. Thirty minutes later, Mrs. Krim burst into the office claiming that Ms. Cartmen had stolen the item from her son and that it was the type of badge everyone was wearing outside of school. The badge was returned to Mrs. Krim, and Kasey did not wear it to school again. However, a copy of the badge was made on the copier in case Mrs. Krim decided to make a larger issue of the incident.

What Should Have Happened and Why

Ms. Cartmen recognized the disruption that the badge caused in the detention room. By calmly demanding the badge and taking control of it without unnecessary embarrassment to herself or Kasey, she took the appropriate action.

Ms. Cartmen also was correct to take the badge to a member of the administration. In _Bethel School District No. 403 v. Fraser,_ 54 Sup. Ct. 5054 (1986), the United States Supreme Court ruled that schools have a higher responsibility in the community and, therefore, should demand and expect more civility within the schools than might be expected in public places other than the school.

Unfortunately, common courtesies and civil respect have eroded in our society. Parents, in many cases, do not feel that schools are any different from a private home, street corner, boardwalk, or mall.

School personnel need to maintain a proper climate and atmosphere within the school, because students may not be immersed in an environment of civility except at school. Often, proper language and respect for all others are taught with consistency only in school. Young people today are bombarded with sex, vulgarity, and disrespectful behavior at home, within their peer groups, and through the media. It is an uphill battle for schools to maintain civility. However, it is a responsibility that cannot be ignored.

"But, Daddy, Everyone Wears Them"

SNAPSHOT 1-2

Cassy Smith is wearing a revealing halter top on a hot day in June. Her English IV teacher, Mr. Lidnar, reports to Mr. Jonas, the vice-principal, that Cassy is distracting the boys in the class, because they are paying more attention to her than they are to Shakespeare's writings. Her halter clearly is in violation of the district dress code policy. Mr. Jonas calls Cassy's home to ask a parent to bring a more appropriate article of clothing to school for Cassy to wear. Within 15 minutes of the call, Mr. Smith is in Mr. Jonas's office demanding to see "that pervert teacher who can't keep his eyes off my little girl."

Main Topic

Civility in school

Subtopics

Dress code

School climate and atmosphere

Sexual behavior

Threats

Possible Solutions

Mr. Jonas should

1. Request that a female staff member observe Cassy's halter top, and judge whether it is a distraction in school.

2. Calm Cassy's dad by explaining that the dress code prohibits halter tops in school and why, and give him a copy of the policy that all parents were asked to sign in September.

3. Bring Cassy's dad to the class to see the teacher in action.

4. Schedule an appointment for all parties to meet after school.

What Would You Do?

_____

_____

_____

_____

_____

What Really Happened

Mr. Lidnar insisted that he have the opportunity to speak to Cassy's dad. The teacher asked the father if he would prefer to have students watching his daughter or the teacher. Cassy's dad agreed that, dressed in the halter top, she probably was a distraction in class, and he apologized to Mr. Lidnar for the negative comments he had made. Cassy did not wear revealing clothing again.

What Should Have Happened and Why

Under the district dress code, a student's clothing or appearance can be a classroom distraction that prevents other students from learning. One way for a teacher to avoid the accusations made by Cassy's dad is to arrange to have a same-gender teacher or nurse report the student who is dressed inappropriately.

Over the years, the courts have ruled that the schools can regulate student dress. To do so, schools must have a reasonable dress code that prohibits clothing that is immodest or disruptive to the educational environment (Parkay & Hardcastle, 1992, pp. 283-284). The courts have also endorsed policies that are designed to protect the health and safety of students (McCarthy & Cambron-McCabe, 1987, p. 130).

"Oh, Yeah? And Your Mother . . . "

Mrs. Calhoun is teaching a social studies class that involves a debatable topic. Two students, Sven and Abdul, take the debate seriously and personally. They begin to raise their voices and to exchange racially loaded epithets. Other students appear to take sides.

Main Topic

Classroom management

Subtopics

Racism

Controversial topics

Possible Solutions

Mrs. Calhoun should

1. Stop the discussion immediately, and use the opportunity to teach a lesson on how to properly approach controversial topics.

2. Hold her breath until she turns blue as a way to remove the attention from Sven and Abdul.

3. Let the discussion go until someone threatens violence.

4. Call for help.

What Would You Do?

_____

_____

_____

_____

_____

What Really Happened

The social studies department chairperson happened to hear the loud voices coming from the classroom as she was walking down the hall. Through her intervention, the emotions were quelled. Mrs. Calhoun's yearly evaluation process included a requirement that she attend a workshop related to the teaching of controversial topics.

What Should Have Happened and Why

Mrs. Calhoun should have been trained to handle such situations through her teacher-education program. Heated debates can easily start, especially in social studies classes. The teacher needs to establish classroom rules and routines that take into account students potentially becoming emotionally and physically upset by selected topics. A quality social studies teacher is able to control such debate and use the overt involvement of the students to strengthen the lesson (Stevens, 1988). Over the past 20 years, social studies texts have become more and more bland, as publishers try to appeal to broad audiences. In turn, the published materials available for teachers have become politically correct to a point at which the emotional context of a historical event is lost. No wonder students find history boring.

Using the professional-development plan to enhance and develop skills in this area is an excellent way to help Mrs. Calhoun become a better teacher. She needs the skills necessary to control such classroom behavior, or students will learn to take advantage of her weakness and steer her away from the curriculum whenever they get the opportunity. This incident should be a warning sign to her to obtain the training as soon as possible. The United States Department of Education has identified the need for teachers to obtain career-long professional development at all levels of education (United States Department of Education, 1997).

"I Can Take Him Any Day"

SNAPSHOT
1-4

Mr. DeFeo, a high school physical education teacher, prides himself in keeping trim and healthy. He recently obtained his black belt in karate, a great honor and accomplishment for a 50-year-old man. One of his students, Nick Jeroff, refuses to believe Mr. DeFeo was able to earn such status and challenges him in front of the class. Nick rushes him and tries to punch him in the face. Mr. DeFeo sidesteps Nick and flips him to the floor, grabs Nick's arm, twists it to render him immobile, and then kicks him several times in the side. Nick is removed by an ambulance and is eventually diagnosed as having two broken ribs.

Main Topic

Reasonable force

Subtopics

Safety

Tort liability

Violence in school

Possible Solutions

Mr. DeFeo should

1. Apologize to Nick, and promise it will never happen again.

2. Visit Nick, and promise to do more damage if Nick ever challenges him again.

3. Call his lawyer immediately—he has a huge problem.

4. Try to calm Nick's parents down by explaining how he lost control and promising it will never happen again.

What Would You Do?

_____

_____

_____

_____

_____

What Really Happened

Nick's parents sued Mr. DeFeo and won. His homeowner's insurance paid the settlement. He resigned his teaching position and opened a karate school in another state.

What Should Have Happened and Why

Teachers must recognize that limited restraint is the behavioral expectation for teachers. Students may be restrained if they are in the process of harming the teacher, another student, or themselves, or are damaging school property. However, the limit on physical contact is restraint of the student, not punishment or inflicting injury beyond the restraint. Mr. DeFeo was absolutely wrong to accept the physical challenge from the student in this situation, and he paid the price. Teachers are supposed to be above such behavior and to be able to resist the temptation to become physically involved in fighting a student. Teachers who even consider such action need to seek help and counseling.

The Chemistry Class Nightmare

Mr. Carter is teaching a chemistry class. His attention is focused on two other students when Josh Noble drops a hot beaker on the lab desk and cuts himself on the arm. He is bleeding profusely. Several students panic and begin to scream.

Main Topic

Safety

Possible Solutions

Mr. Carter should

1. Call the office immediately and ask for help.

2. Give Josh a paper towel, and order all students out of the room.

3. Immediately order students away from Josh so that he can breathe.

4. Use universal precautions to help Josh and protect himself in the process.

What Would You Do?

_____

_____

_____

_____

_____

What Really Happened

The incident was treated as an accident, and Mr. Carter reacted quickly and appropriately to tend to Josh's injury.

What Should Have Happened and Why

Mr. Carter was appropriately trained to use first aid and universal precautions when contacting any body fluids. Universal precautions are the precautions that school personnel are required to follow when cleaning up body fluids or helping a student who, for example, has vomited or is bleeding. The teacher should use latex gloves (which should be in the teacher's desk) and a chlorine-bleach solution to clean up the area where blood or any other body fluid has fallen. Accidents are not limited to the science classroom or shop classes. Every teacher needs to have a working knowledge of first aid and of universal precautions. Teachers must educate themselves and question the administration of their district about the resources available in an emergency and the use of such precautions. Most districts will have policies in place requiring teacher participation in staff-development activities that relate to student safety and protection. A working communication system needs to be in place so that medical help can be called in an emergency. Teachers need to know the location of emergency equipment such as fire extinguishers and medical kits.

Teachers need to remain calm and under control even during emergencies. Not only do teachers need to take care of an injured student, but they also need to make sure all the other students remain out of harm's way. Sending students out of the room does not permit their ongoing supervision. By identifying leaders from the very beginning of the year and being prepared for such emergencies, holding practice emergency drills, and making a routine out of handling possible emergencies, calm will prevail and students will react within reason.

References

McCarthy, M., & Cambron-McCabe, N. (1987). *Public school law: Teachers' and students' rights.* Newton, MA: Allyn & Bacon.

Parkay, F., & Hardcastle, S. B. (1992). *Becoming a teacher* (2nd ed., annotated instructor's edition). Needham Heights, MA: Allyn & Bacon.

Stevens, M. (1988). *The effective teaching review manual.* Pittsford, NY: Stevens.

United States Department of Education. (1997). *Building knowledge for a nation of learners: A framework for education research 1997.* Washington, DC: U.S. Government Printing Office.

Confronting Student Behavior Outside the Classroom

"What Are You Doing Here?"

SNAPSHOT 2-1

Ms. Smart is a new teacher. She enters the girl's lavatory and finds two students, Mary and a boy whose name she does not know, in a stall together. The boy refuses to leave when Ms. Smart asks him to accompany her to the office. He calmly states that there are no prohibitions listed in the student handbook against students entering the lavatory of the opposite sex. Ms. Smart knows that if she leaves, he will escape.

Main Topic

Decision making

Subtopics

Sexual behavior

Policy

Possible Solutions

Ms. Smart should

1. Tell Mary to go to the office to have an administrator come to the lavatory.

2. Tell the boy to leave immediately and never to enter the girls' lavatory again.

3. Stand in the doorway to prevent either student from leaving, and wait for another staff member to send an administrator to the lavatory.

4. Laugh at the situation, turn Mary in for a cut of class, and let Mary tell the vice-principal who the boy is.

What Would You Do?

_____

_____

_____

_____

_____

What Really Happened

The teacher kept her cool and stood in the doorway of the lavatory until another teacher came by. The second teacher went to the office to obtain help for the teacher. Steve was suspended for being in an obviously unauthorized area, and the handbook for the next school year contained a statement that separated lavatories by gender.

What Should Have Happened and Why

Teachers must be prepared to make an attempt to obtain help and secure the area, identify the students involved, and report an incident in writing to the administration.

Ms. Smart handled this situation extremely well. Students are acutely aware that teachers are at a total disadvantage when the teacher does not know the name of the student. Getting to know the names of your students as soon as possible is very important in establishing rapport and control of the classroom. In a situation in which you will be in a common area, such as the cafeteria or hallway, make every effort to find a member of the staff who can identify a student if necessary. Unfortunately, yearbooks can also become mug books, and identifying a student through the use of the yearbook is prudent in some cases. Although it is a controversial practice, many schools provide copies of yearbooks to local police departments for such purposes.

In response to complaints from Steve and his parents, the administration made sure that the separation by gender of lavatories and locker rooms was clearly stated in the next edition of the student handbook. Although school officials may take such separation for granted, students may observe coed bathrooms in movies as well as female sports reporters in the locker room interviewing male players after a game. Nonetheless, the faculty had not believed Steve was confused, and now the handbook is clear on this matter.

"Does a Flush Beat a Full House?"

While chaperoning the senior trip to Florida, Mr. Dingman was conducting the standard evening bed check when he discovered a heavy poker game in one of the rooms. There was over $400 in the pot. The students invited him to join in.

Main Topic

Gambling

Subtopic

Extension of school authority

Possible Solutions

Mr. Dingman should

1. Join the game.

2. Order the game shut down.

3. Take the money and return it to the parents.

4. Report the incident to the administrator in charge, so she will handle it.

What Would You Do?

_____

_____

_____

_____

_____

What Really Happened

Mr. Dingman shut the game down immediately. He divided the money evenly among the players and ordered the students not to play again, or he would report them to the administration. To his knowledge, the students did not play poker again on the trip.

What Should Have Happened and Why

Under similar circumstances, teachers must make sure that they are not perceived as being involved in the game. Having another faculty member witness the disbursement of the money and having students sign receipts for the returned money are good tactics.

Most school districts have policies that prohibit gambling by students. Recent studies have shown that gambling is an addiction and that young people are not immune to the temptations of gambling. An excellent source for information on the subject is www.nati.org/teens.htm.

Students generally do not recognize their actions as possible signs of a gambling problem. When students observe teachers filling in weekly football pools and making references to casinos, they are able to draw a positive connection to the behavior and consider it acceptable. Especially susceptible are students who live with geographical access to casinos, racetracks, and other sites at which gambling is legal.

An effective teacher recognizes the danger signals of such student behavior and seeks help for any students involved.

By condoning the card game, Mr. Dingman would have placed himself in jeopardy, because the students were violating the district policy. He should also have reported the incident to the administration for disciplinary action.

An excellent Web site for information related to gambling as an addiction for all groups, including adolescents, is Gamblers Anonymous at www.macad.org/referral/directory/.

SNAPSHOT 2-3

"And the Line Is Packers by Seven"

Monday mornings during the fall, Mr. Lithman notices that Jim Greese is a popular young man in the cafeteria before school starts. He notices Jim giving money to a different group of students each week. By asking several students with whom he has a good relationship, Mr. Lithman finds out that Jim is running a large football pool and that several members of the staff participate.

Main Topic

Gambling

Subtopics

Trust

Staff impropriety

Possible Solutions

Mr. Lithman should

1. Tell the other staff members to get out of the pool.

2. Turn the matter over to the administration.

3. Recommend that the president of the teachers' union tell the other staff members to get out of the pool.

4. Call Jim's parents, and inform them of the situation.

What Would You Do?

_____

_____

_____

_____

_____

What Really Happened

Mr. Lithman approached a few members of the staff who were involved in the pool. Through their intervention, the pool was closed down and Jim Greese took his business off campus without any teacher involvement.

What Should Have Happened and Why

Under similar circumstances, the teacher must be prepared to be assertive and reject peer pressure to go along with an illegal activity.

Mr. Lithman probably prevented a scandal within the school, which would have resulted if news of the pool and the involvement of staff members had been reported to the police or media. But he was taking a chance, because his actions could have been interpreted by many staff members as interfering in something that was none of his business. He should have confidentially reported the incident to the administration. And Jim's counselor should help him face the negative and illegal aspects of his behavior. Jim's parents also need to know about this incident.

Generally, most members of boards of education are members of the community who are conservative and religious by nature and predilection. This type of behavior on the part of students and staff members can result in disciplinary action against the student and charges of conduct unbecoming a teacher against members of the staff who were involved. When in doubt, teachers should err on the conservative side instead of taking the chance of being caught up in a potentially danger-ous professional circumstance.

Nudity.com

Ms. Travers hears in the teachers' room that someone programmed the computers in the business department to call up a pornographic Web site when they were switched on. Later, she overhears a conversation between two students in the media center identifying Alice Monroe as the student responsible for this prank. Alice is the valedictorian of the senior class and president of the student council and has a reputation for being a Goody Two-shoes.

Main Topic

Sexual behavior

Subtopics

Rumors

Teacher responsibility

Possible Solutions

Ms. Travers should

1. Confront Alice, and ask her if the rumor is true.

2. Report the rumor to the administration.

3. Go to the media center to see if she can find some evidence that points to Alice.

4. Ignore the rumor, because Alice is not the kind of student who would ever do such a thing.

What Would You Do?

_____

_____

_____

_____

_____

What Really Happened

The rumor was true about the Web site. However, Alice had nothing to do with the automatic accessing of the site. The media technician checked the log-on codes and computer history and discovered that another student was responsible. That student was suspended and, as a result of the board's appropriate-use policy, was banned from using any computers in the school; the ban extended until the student graduated.

What Should Have Happened and Why

Schools are the largest rumor mills in any town. Students like Alice are sometimes the target of rumors because of their status within the student culture. Before making accusations, teachers have a responsibility to maintain discretion when rumors are forthcoming and to make attempts to find out if such rumors are true. A fair warning to all teachers: Be acutely aware of comments and rumors that are spread in the teachers' lounge. Taking such comments with a grain of salt is a good approach.

Photos at Eleven

Rich Bond is a student in Mr. Albert's high school English IV class. One morning after class, Mr. Albert notices a folder has been left under Rich's desk on the book rack. As he picks it up, several photographs fall out. The photos show

Rich and another student, Janice Wold, in the nude, making love. Additional students, whom Mr. Albert recognizes, are in the background watching Rich and Janice.

Main Topic

Sexual behavior

Subtopics

Civility in school

Search and seizure

Possible Solutions

Mr. Albert should

1. Put the pictures back in the folder, return the folder to Rich, and pretend he never saw them.
2. Call the parents of each student, and present the photos to them.
3. Make copies of the photos in case he loses them.
4. Turn the matter over to the administration.

What Would You Do?

_____

_____

_____

_____

_____

What Really Happened

Mr. Albert claims he threw the photos into the incinerator immediately after finding them. However, other copies of the photos found their way into the hands of a local reporter, and they became the scandal of the year in the community. Reputations of individuals and families were destroyed.

Because no school rules were broken, the school did not take any action against the students. The school district did offer counseling to all the students involved. Rich mentioned that he had left copies in his classroom and did not know what had happened to them, thus making others suspicious of Mr. Albert and the possibility that he possessed copies. Mr. Albert is asked repeatedly by other teachers and friends if they can look at the photographs.

What Should Have Happened and Why

Teachers must be prepared to turn lewd materials found in school over to the administration, with a detailed written explanation of how they were found. This must be done as soon as possible. No teachers want to have this type of material found in their possession under any circumstances.

Adolescents, unfortunately, are subjected to the sexually explicit materials that exist in society today. Teachers need to be aware of the pressure, most notably peer pressure, on students to become sexually active. By setting an example in their demeanor, dress, and use of language, teachers are the final bastions of civility in the lives of many students. Trying to prevent students from hearing and seeing sexually graphic material and becoming curious about it is tantamount to using a teaspoon to stop the tide from coming in. However, when the opportunity presents itself to teach abstinence or set an appropriate example, teachers across the curriculum should seize the teaching opportunity.

Hooky and Ladder

SNAPSHOT 2-6

In mid-May, the Statewide Firemen's Convention is held in a nearby city during an extended weekend. Mr. Snyder, a custodian in the school, tells Mr. Levy, a teacher, that Allen Smith, a student, attended the convention with his parents. Allen was to have taken a major test in Mr. Levy's class that day. Allen has been absent numerous times and is on the borderline of failing for the school year. His mother called the school office on the morning of the test day saying his uncle had passed away, and so he would not be in school. She wanted Allen to take his test the next day.

Main Topic

Truancy

Subtopics

Parental reaction

Grading policies

Possible Solutions

Mr. Levy should

1. Give Allen the chance to take the test, because his parents forced him to go to the convention, and it is not the child's fault.

2. Request a parent conference with Mrs. Smith, and confront her with Mr. Snyder's observation.

3. Give Allen an F on the test until he provides proof of his uncle's passing.

4. Turn the whole matter over to the administration.

What Would You Do?

_____

_____

_____

_____

_____

What Really Happened

Mr. Levy refused to allow Allen to take the test until he produced evidence of his uncle's passing. Mr. and Mrs. Smith became enraged with Mr. Levy and accused him of being prejudiced against their son due to his color. A hearing was held at the superintendent's level, and the Smiths refused to provide the requested documentation.

Mr. and Mrs. Smith were eventually brought to municipal court for their failure to send Allen to school. They were fined $75 a day for each day they could not produce legitimate documentation for their son's absences, going back to the beginning of the school year. The fine was suspended. Allen was not absent for the remainder of the year.

What Should Have Happened and Why

Teachers must maintain impeccable classroom attendance records. These records are official and may be requested by the administration or a court of law. The administration could not reason with or convince the Smiths through meetings, counseling—or threats of detentions or suspension for Allen—that there is great value in attending school. Unfortunately, parents find it very easy to make racial accusations against teachers, especially when they are trying to deflect attention away from their children. In this case, the teacher had kept excellent records, and most people interpreted the racial accusation as unsupported.

By bringing the issue to court, the district clearly proclaimed to the community that they were going to enforce the law, and the parents discovered that this was a serious matter and the judge could impose a financial burden on them for their failure to send their son to school.

The Cheerleader

Mr. Webster is the vice-principal. Roland Mapps is absent on the day of a major-league sports parade in a nearby city. His mother has called to say Roland has a dental emergency. While watching the news in the teachers' workroom during lunch, Mr. Webster notices that Roland is clearly visible holding a bottle of beer, wearing his school jacket, and cheering for the team. Hoping the TV station will repeat their report on the evening news, Mr. Webster videotapes the six o'clock broadcast, and the footage is repeated.

Main Topic

Truancy

Subtopics

Parental reaction

Substance abuse

Possible Solutions

Mr. Webster should

1. Suspend Roland after showing the mother the newscast.

2. Speak to Roland privately, show him the newscast, and give him a chance to talk to his mother first.

3. Ignore the newscast, and take the mother's word, because she doesn't seem to care.

4. Suspend Roland, and show the newscast to the board of education as a surprise, because he will look good to them for doing this and because Mrs. Mapps will probably appeal the suspension.

What Would You Do?

_____

_____

_____

_____

_____

What Really Happened

Roland was suspended, because it was his third truancy of the year. His mother appealed the suspension but dropped the appeal when the family dentist refused to provide written documentation of Roland's dental work. Mrs. Mapps continuously berated Mr. Webster in public. She even ran for election to the board of education on the platform of removing him from his position. She abruptly ended her campaign against Mr. Webster when her son graduated.

What Should Have Happened and Why

Roland should have been suspended, and the administration should have maintained the high road while imposing the suspension. The actions of a parent should not become the major factor when working with a student. As much as it would have been satisfying to the administration to embarrass Mrs. Mapps, it would have served no purpose in teaching Roland the value and importance of attending school on a regular basis.

Students are placed in a precarious position when given the opportunity to break rules knowing that their parents will back them up if they are caught. The lesson needs to be absorbed by the student, and conditions need to be established that would encourage students like Roland to attend school, because they need an education.

Parents like Mrs. Mapps are very difficult to work with. They do not believe the school has any authority over their child. They can also say anything they want in public. In contrast, teachers and district employees must remain professional and refrain from counterattacks. The one saving fact is that most people like Mrs. Mapps disappear from the school scene as soon as their child is no longer in school or the family moves to another district.

SNAPSHOT 2-8

Show and Tell

Mr. Eastman has heard that one of the history teachers was encouraging students to bring in World War II relics. As he walks past a student's locker, he observes what appears to be the handle of a pistol on the top shelf of Kim Randall's locker just as Kim slams and locks the locker door.

Main Topic

Weapons

Subtopics

Search and seizure

Rumors

School climate and atmosphere

Possible Solutions

Mr. Eastman should

1. Ignore the gun, because he has heard that a teacher was asking students to bring in relics from the war.

2. Report the incident to the administration immediately.

3. Wait for another teacher to pass by who can stand guard until an administrator can come to open the door.

4. Grab the student, and force him to go to the office immediately.

What Would You Do?

_____

_____

_____

_____

_____

What Really Happened

Mr. Eastman found another teacher to guard the locker while he went to find Kim and take her to the office. Kim voluntarily opened her locker, and a gun was inside.

The gun was real, and a teacher had asked for relics. The student's grandfather had removed the firing pin and rendered the weapon harmless. Looking at the gun from a distance, no one would know that it had been disabled. A school official asked the history teacher not to request such items in the future, and the administration praised Mr. Eastman for being so observant. Because Kim was following the history teacher's request, no administrative action was taken against her.

What Should Have Happened and Why

This incident took place in the mid-1970s. Due to recent events, the issue would become much more serious today.

Teachers should never encourage students to bring weapons to school under any circumstances. To do so is conduct unbecoming a teacher, and severe disciplinary sanctions can result.

Students should be aware of the danger of bringing weapons to school, and parents should not allow their children to possess such items. Students could be suspended for at least one year, and criminal charges might be filed against them.

Zero tolerance for weapons on school property needs to be enforced everywhere for the protection of all members of the educational community.

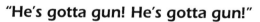

SNAPSHOT 2-9

"He's gotta gun! He's gotta gun!"

Mr. Alexander and Ms. Conover are standing in the courtyard of the Marriott, right outside Disney World, on the first evening of the senior trip. They have over 300 students in their care, and they are commenting on how well behaved the students have been so far. All of a sudden, Judy Blanchard comes running up to them yelling, "He'sgottagun!" repeatedly. The two chaperones calm Judy down, and she explains that a local resident had tried to pick up girls from the class and had been rejected. He left them, returned several minutes later, and pointed a rifle out his car window at the girls.

Main Topic

Weapons

Subtopics

Threats

Possible Solutions

The Chaperones should

1. Call Judy's parents.

2. Contact the police.

3. Check the location of every student to make sure the gunman did not force someone to go with him in his car.

4. Remember that Judy has a great sense of humor, and go along with her joke.

What Would You Do?

_____

_____

_____

_____

_____

What Really Happened?

A local man was indeed rejected by the girls and did point a gun at the students. The chaperones contacted the police and also made sure each student was accounted for. The state police took 45 minutes to arrive at the hotel and another 2 hours to discover that the gunman, who knew the hotel manager, was sitting in the lobby. He was arrested and charged with reckless display of a firearm. He was eventually sentenced to two years of confinement in a state mental health facility.

What Should Have Happened and Why

One never knows when the threat of, or the actual appearance of, a weapon will crash in on the environment. "Be prepared" is the only advice to give teachers under such circumstances. Students need to know their limits and what the teachers in charge expect of them. In the senior-trip incident, if discipline had been lax and if students had not been where they were supposed to be, this situation could have been much worse. In the 2 hours and 45 minutes that the gunman was unaccounted for, the teachers and students felt a great deal of stress and fear. Luckily, no one was hurt.

"What Would It Take . . . "

Mr. Ogle, the vice-principal, is chaperoning a dance. He checks the parking lot and finds a case of beer in plain view in the back seat of Julie Johnson's car. He asks Julie to go to the office with him to call her parents. He also signals to Mrs. Schell to follow them to the office. When they get to the office, Julie begins to unbutton her blouse and comments that she would do "anything" not to have her parents find out about the beer. When Mrs. Schell clears her throat to indicate her presence in the room, Julie stops abruptly and quickly buttons her blouse.

SNAPSHOT 2-10

Main Topic

Sexual conduct

Subtopics

Substance abuse

Due process

Possible Solutions

Mr. Ogle should

1. Take Julie up on her offer.
2. Stop Julie immediately, and walk out of the office.
3. Call Julie's parents, and tell them they must come to the office immediately, because their daughter is making sexual advances and has beer in her possession.
4. Protest loudly against Julie's advances so that Mrs. Schell can quote him if the incident causes him trouble.

What Would You Do?

_____

_____

_____

_____

_____

What Really Happened

Luckily, the vice-principal asked a female chaperone to follow him to his office, and her appearance ended Julie's inappropriate behavior toward him. A school official contacted Julie's parents, and they came to the school immediately. Mr. Ogle told them about the beer in Julie's car but made no mention of Julie's seductive behavior. Later, however, Mrs. Schell mentioned the incident confidentially to Julie's guidance counselor.

What Should Have Happened and Why

Teachers and administrators must constantly be aware of the possibility of a student making an inappropriate offer or accusation. Always leave a door open when alone with a student, regardless of gender, or have another adult present to avoid the perception of any wrongdoing.

Whether school authorities should have told Julie's parents about her inappropriate actions with Mr. Ogle is debatable. The incident could have turned into a *he said, she said* situation if Julie had denied doing anything wrong. Moreover, if school authorities had reported her actions to her parents, she might have claimed that she was misinterpreted or that Mr. Ogle was the one who became flirtatious. Either way, the vice-principal would have been in a precarious situation. School personnel must always be above reproach when speaking with students, especially when any sexual comments, jokes, or references are made.

Playing Suckface

Ms. Kimmel is a teacher in a high school. As she is walking toward class, she turns the corner and finds a male and a female student kissing passionately.

Main Topic

Civility in school

Subtopics

Sexual conduct

School climate and atmosphere

Parental reaction

Possible Solutions

Ms. Kimmel should

1. Shake her head as she tapped the female student on the shoulder, indicating that school is not the place for such kissing.

2. Loudly state that she forgot her crowbar this morning, and the two students should separate on their own.

3. Report the students to the office.

4. Counsel the female student about public displays of affection the next time she sees her alone.

What Would You Do?

_____

_____

_____

_____

_____

What Really Happened

The students were brought to the office. Ms. Kimmel insisted the male student call the father of the female student. The male student refused to call and asked to see his guidance counselor. Through the intervention of a counselor, the students were assigned after-school detentions, and the parents were not contacted. The principal instructed Ms. Kimmel not to make such requests in the future. Because a district policy prohibits public displays of affection, her job is to report the incident and allow the administration to follow through with students and parents.

What Should Have Happened and Why

The male student was correct in not calling the female student's father. The only people who have legal standing in any disciplinary matter are a student's own parents. The teacher should have reported the incident to the administration in written form, and the district policy for public displays of affection should have been enforced. These types of actions on the part of students disrupt the educational process, demean each student involved, and negatively affect the school climate. The counselor should have contacted the parents of each student to report both the incident and the fact that the students were assigned to detention as a result of the kiss. Parents have a right to know when these types of situations occur. In many cases, but not all, the parents will reinforce the discipline at home.

Moreover, by asking the male student to telephone the father of the female student, the teacher was guilty of applying a sexual stereotype.

Working With Administrators and Colleagues

3

"Do You Want This Whole Town to Hate You?"

SNAPSHOT 3-1

Tony Armstrong, the all-everything running back for the football team, is acting in a very suspicious manner during Mr. Ross's test. After class, Mr. Ross (a new teacher) looks closely around Tony's desk and finds several Post-it notes stuck under the desktop with crib notes for the test. Mr. Ross reports this event to Mr. Rahwah, the vice-principal. Just as the dismissal bell sounds for the end of the day, the football coach storms into Mr. Ross's class to inform him that Tony is going to play in the championship game on Saturday, because this whole event is going to be forgotten.

Main Topic

Cheating

Subtopics

Politics

Grading policies

Possible Solutions

Mr. Ross should

1. Walk out of the room immediately to avoid confronting the coach.

2. Engage the coach in a professional dialogue to convince the coach of the virtue of honesty in his players.

3. Use the intercom system to call for administrative help.

4. Take the threat seriously, and file a grievance against the coach.

What Would You Do?

_____

_____

_____

_____

_____

What Really Happened

Tony did not play in the game. Mr. Ross tried to discuss the issue with the coach, who was disappointed that Mr. Ross could not see his way to downplaying the cheating incident and giving Tony a chance to take a retest. The coach and Mr. Ross have not spoken to each other for over ten years. Mr. Ross and the vice-principal had a rocky relationship after the incident, too. Although the accusation was unspoken, those in the school who were gung ho about the sports program considered Mr. Ross to be antiathletics.

What Should Have Happened and Why

Mr. Ross was correct to apply the school policy about cheating. By trying to engage the coach in a professional dialogue, Mr. Ross was demonstrating his integrity and strength of character as a new teacher. And he rejected the pressure to provide a special standard for student athletes.

Teachers need to recognize that members of the same faculty will have conflicts and differences of philosophy. In this case, those members of the faculty, including the vice-principal, who agree with the coach will apply peer pressure to challenge Mr. Ross's strength and integrity. Mr. Ross needs to recognize that many others, most of whom will remain silent in this case, agree with him. He did well to resist this pressure and maintain his position.

Inquiring People . . .

SNAPSHOT 3-2

Ms. Hoyne, a young teacher whose classroom is next to the classroom of recently divorced Joe Perno, seems to be constantly in his company. She has "inadvertently" brushed against him at the copier, solicited private information about his personal life, and whispered to him that she is not wearing underwear on various days. Rumors have begun to spread among students and staff that they are an item.

Main Topic

Rumors

Subtopic

Teacher as public persona

Possible Solutions

Mr. Perno should

1. Ask Ms. Hoyne out.

2. Tell her to leave him alone, because he does not mix his social life with his business life.

3. Ask another teacher to tell Ms. Hoyne that he has another girlfriend.

4. Request that an administrator tell Ms. Hoyne that her behavior is not considered appropriate in school.

What Would You Do?

_____

_____

_____

_____

_____

What Really Happened

The two teachers involved in this snapshot eventually married.

What Should Have Happened and Why

Teachers need to be acutely aware of their visibility within the community. Less than 100 years ago, teachers signed contracts that included behavior clauses. Although an enlightenment of sorts has occurred during the past 40 years, teachers are still held up to more stringent standards than other members of society are. Teachers who are involved in minor incidents that have a hint of negative morality or even unlawfulness find they become front-page news very quickly. Avoiding this type of behavior, or even the perception of impropriety, is important in every teacher's life.

"You Are Satisfactory"

SNAPSHOT 3-3

Mr. Bucciero is a first-year teacher who is observed for the first time by Mr. Rappoport, an administrator who is near retirement.

Mr. Bucciero receives **satisfactory** on the evaluation form in all categories. The only comment written on the observation form is that "the shades on the classroom windows should be level across the bottom."

Main Topic

Teacher evaluation

Subtopic

Administrative relations

Possible Solutions

Mr. Bucciero should

1. Bring a copy of the evaluation to the superintendent, and request that a more serious evaluation be conducted.

2. Try to get help from the union president.

3. Nothing—*satisfactory* is a good rating.

4. Write a strong rebuttal pointing out all the positive aspects of the lesson that were ignored.

What Would You Do?

_____

_____

_____

_____

_____

What Really Happened

Mr. Bucciero did nothing about the evaluation. However, several years later, when he applied to another district for an administrative position, he did not get the job. Off the record, a member of the interview committee told him that the committee members felt Mr. Bucciero was hiding something due to the bland evaluation he had received from Mr. Rappoport.

What Should Have Happened and Why

Teachers must realize that their employment record contains mainly the observations and evaluations of members of the administration. Teachers need to have a working knowledge of the evaluation process and use it to showcase their skills for future reference. Teachers should not fear observations. They should welcome them as opportunities to show off their preparation, presentation, and teaching skills.

The maintenance of a professional file and portfolio is highly recommended. Include observations, any awards or honors received, photographs of special events in the classroom, exceptional lesson plans, newspaper coverage of special events, and notes from parents. One never knows when circumstances will shift, and the need to apply for a teaching position or a different position in education will arise. A solid portfolio that clearly describes the type of teacher you are can be invaluable when applying for and interviewing for a new position. Teachers cannot predict the future, and, although they feel they will never leave their present district, they must be prepared to obtain another position if circumstances warrant.

SNAPSHOT 3-4

Is White Collar Crime Really a Crime?

One day, Mr. Miller asks Mr. Atwater, a new teacher at West High School, for a ride to school because his car is being repaired. While he is waiting for Mr. Miller, Mrs. Miller offers Mr. Atwater a seat in the family room. Mr. Atwater can't help but notice the entertainment center that Mr. Miller has built. Looking closely at the center, Mr. Atwater sees a VCR and a television set clearly marked "Property of West High School."

Main Topic

Ethics

Subtopic

Staff impropriety

Possible Solutions

Mr. Atwater should

1. Report his observation to the administration immediately on arrival at school.

2. Mention to Mr. Miller what he saw, and hope a valid explanation follows.

3. Ask an older member of the staff if any items have been missing from the audiovisual department.

4. Pretend he never saw any of the items; it is none of his business.

What Would You Do?

_____

_____

_____

_____

_____

What Really Happened

Mr. Atwater asked the business administrator, in a very round-about way, how the district discarded items that were replaced by newer models. He discovered through these conversations that Mr. Miller had purchased some audiovisual equipment at the last auction offered by the district.

What Should Have Happened and Why

Mr. Atwater did the right thing by not jumping to conclusions. In similar situations, teachers need at least to take at face value the honesty, integrity, and professionalism of their fellow teachers. In this case, it is not Mr. Atwater's responsibility to act as a policeman. However, if he suspects that Mr. Miller is not being honest, he needs to be sure that he is not connected with him in any manner until he no longer suspects his colleague of dishonesty. Mr. Atwater should not develop a close friendship with Mr. Miller if he distrusts him.

Slow Dance

Mr. Polland is the principal of a midsize high school. On the Monday following the prom, Mr. Ganges, father of Alyssa, a senior, barges into his office to complain that the class advisor, Mr. Harmon, acted inappropriately when he danced with Alyssa at the prom. They danced a slow dance, and his hand wandered to the top of her buttocks where he allegedly squeezed her repeatedly during the dance.

Main Topic

Teacher as public persona

Subtopics

Sexual behavior

Staff impropriety

Possible Solutions

Mr. Polland should

1. Bring Mr. Harmon in to join the meeting and explain himself.

2. Call the school attorney to ask for advice.

3. Ask to speak to Alyssa to get her first-person story.

4. Promise to discipline Mr. Harmon, and begin to write a policy to prohibit dancing with students by staff members.

What Would You Do?

_____

_____

_____

_____

_____

What Really Happened

Mr. Polland promised Mr. Ganges that he would investigate the matter. He then spoke to Mr. Harmon. Mr. Harmon denied the allegation. Mr. Polland also spoke to all the teachers who attended the prom and found that none of them had observed anything that would verify Mr. Ganges's story. Finally, he spoke to Alyssa, who admitted that she had a crush on Mr. Harmon and told some of her friends that he had squeezed her when they were dancing. One of her friends had relayed the story to Mr. Ganges. Mr. Ganges and Mr. Polland met with Alyssa, and she repeated her story to her dad. Mr. Ganges was unhappy with his daughter but felt she was telling the truth now, and no action should be taken against Mr. Harmon.

What Should Have Happened and Why

Mr. Polland did an excellent job investigating this allegation. He did so quietly and effectively. He also developed a policy proposal, which was eventually adopted by the board of education, that prohibited dancing or any other physical contact between staff members and students at any social event. Allowing physical contact is clearly not worth the possible aggravation that dancing or even hugging a student can lead to. Students do not need to have school personnel as friends. The adults should maintain a distance befitting their positions of authority. School personnel also do not need to have adolescent friends.

4 Dealing With Parents and the Community

"But I Do Have to Go Now"

Mrs. Mills, a parent of a student in Mrs. Apple's class, appears in her classroom each morning. Mrs. Mills is very concerned about and interested in her son's education. She keeps Mrs. Apple talking in the hallway for 10 to 15 minutes into the class period. Mrs. Mills has Mrs. Apple faxing a progress report to her daily. Mrs. Apple finds herself being distracted from the needs of the other students in her class.

Main Topic

Parental involvement

Subtopic

Teacher responsibility

Possible Solutions

Mrs. Apple should

1. Look at her watch, and act surprised, then tell Mrs. Mills she must attend to her class.

2. Inform the administration about this parent, and request intervention.

3. Politely but firmly tell Mrs. Mills that parent-teacher conferences must be scheduled away from school instructional time.

4. Recognize how important it is to keep parents informed, and continue to meet with Mrs. Mills.

What Would You Do?

_____

_____

_____

_____

_____

What Really Happened

Mrs. Apple could not bring herself to appear as rude to Mrs. Mills. The principal noticed this situation and became involved to the point at which he ordered Mrs. Apple to meet with Mrs. Mills before or after school only. He emphasized that Mrs. Mills could only have appointments with staff members after school, and he imposed time limits on the length of the meetings. The daily fax reports were eliminated, but a weekly progress report was provided in their place.

What Should Have Happened and Why

More things are worth learning than we have time to teach. Limited classroom time should be used efficiently (Brophy, 2000, p. 5). Time spent on tasks is critical to a successful classroom experience for teachers and students. Mrs. Apple also has a contractual obligation to the district to teach her class when scheduled. Mrs. Mills was being selfish and overbearing and had to be stopped.

"My Son Only Played in Half the Quarters"

SNAPSHOT 4-2

Mr. Blake, coach of the high school's male soccer team, is warned by one of the parents of a team member that he should attend the next board of education meeting. He does so, and, during the public portion of the meeting, Mr. Hale, a well-known junior-soccer-league coach and a parent of a member of Mr. Blake's team, launches into a tirade about Mr. Blake's lack of coaching abilities. Despite warnings from the board solicitor and other members of the board, the board president allows Mr. Hale to finish his statements. A local reporter is covering the meeting and reports the story in the paper the next day with banner headlines.

Main Topic

Politics

Subtopics

Teacher as public persona

Due process

Possible Solutions

Mr. Blake should

1. Resign his coaching position, because it is not worth the aggravation he is getting.

2. Submit a letter to the editor exposing Mr. Hale's faults to the public.

3. Organize a parent group to fight the accusations.

4. Bring suit against the board of education for failure to provide due process.

What Would You Do?

_____

_____

_____

_____

_____

What Really Happened

Mr. Blake submitted his resignation as the coach.

What Should Have Happened and Why

In this case, the superintendent of schools or board president ought to have followed the advice of the solicitor and to have stopped Mr. Hale from making his comments. As a result of their inaction, a quality coach was no longer willing to help young people develop their athletic skills, and the students lost a role model and mentor.

In most districts, a complaint procedure is part of policy, or the agreement with the teachers' association outlines procedures that all people must follow to bring a complaint against any employee of the district. Generally, these procedures involve the complainant meeting with the teacher to try to resolve the issue at the lowest possible level. If that meeting is unsuccessful, the complaint moves up the chain of command and, eventually, will be settled by an administrative law judge or in a court of law. At least the procedure requires that complaints be submitted in writing and that evidence be logically presented. All teachers need to know and understand this policy and the chain of command in place for their district.

Coaches are constantly in the limelight. Upset parents and players can use rumor and accusation to destroy a coach, but confidentiality and professional standards generally bind the coach. Some districts require parents to attend special programs on sportsmanship prior to attending games and contests. Being a coach in modern times is an often difficult position, not only because of the challenge of teaching the game or sport but also because they must deal with parents who have unrealistic and inflated images of their children's abilities.

Teachers considering coaching responsibilities need to know the extent to which the athletic program has developed policies and procedures for communication with parents and spectators.

" . . . But Mr. O'Hagan, the Lines Were Soooo Long"

While chaperoning a trip out of town, Mr. O'Hagan is paged and asked to report to the security station in the museum that his class is visiting. He is shown a video of one of his students, Donna Dorfman, shoplifting several items from the gift shop. Donna is the daughter of a member of the board of education.

Main Topic

Politics

Subtopic

Extension of school authority

Possible Solutions

Mr. O'Hagan should

1. Ask the security police to arrest Donna.

2. Offer to take Donna into his custody, and leave the museum immediately.

3. Phone Donna's mother, and have her come to pick Donna up.

4. Offer to pay for the items, and have the charges dropped.

What Would You Do?

_____

_____

_____

_____

_____

What Really Happened

Mr. O'Hagan removed Donna from the museum, which satisfied the museum director. The incident was reported to the administration, and Donna was suspended. Her mother was so embarrassed that she never spoke of the incident to anyone connected with the school.

What Should Have Happened and Why

Mr. O'Hagan behaved commendably. Recognizing the political sensitivity of the issue and the potential embarrassment for Donna and her mother, he kept the situation under control by taking Donna out of the museum. At the same time, he recognized that no one connected with the school should give Donna privileged treatment. Members of the board of education and the staff must be careful not to permit any perception of favoritism for relatives of board members.

"He's a Fine Young Man . . . "

SNAPSHOT 4-4

As Mr. Anderson is teaching his first period class one day, the superintendent of schools comes into the classroom and offers to cover for him while he goes to his office to meet with a parent. In his office, Mr. Anderson finds Mr. Snodgrass, the president of the board of education, waiting. Mr. Snodgrass begins to grill Mr. Anderson about the poor grade he assigned to his son last marking period.

Main Topic

Politics

Subtopic

Grading policies

Possible Solutions

Mr. Anderson should

1. Refuse to speak to Mr. Snodgrass without representation from the union.

2. Obtain copies of work submitted by Mr. Snodgrass's son, and prove that the grade he received was correct.

3. Apologize and raise the grade, hoping Mr. Snodgrass will remember this gesture should there ever be a time the favor can be returned.

4. Invite Mr. Snodgrass to visit his son's class to observe his performance.

What Would You Do?

_____

_____

_____

_____

_____

What Really Happened

Mr. Anderson was well prepared and offered several examples of work that Mr. Snodgrass's son had submitted. Mr. Snodgrass and his son then met with Mr. Anderson after school, and the father supported

Mr. Anderson's position. Several years later, when Mr. Anderson applied for the position of assistant principal, Mr. Snodgrass was his greatest supporter on the board. Mr. Anderson was appointed to the position. Mr. Snodgrass's admiring remarks about Mr. Anderson's professionalism were often quoted.

What Should Have Happened and Why

Teachers must be prepared to recognize each child as an equal in class. That a child is the son or daughter of a member of the board of education is irrelevant. If members of the board pressure teachers to show favoritism toward their children, that is a breach of ethics and can cost the members their seats on the board. To this end, teachers must keep impeccable, unimpeachable records.

Having children of board members in class places additional pressure on teachers. Unfortunately, political pressure does exist, and teachers are not immune to it. The biggest laugh I used to get in teaching educational philosophy was when I would start each class by saying, "There are no politics in education."

"Gotcha"

Vice-principal Alexander is convinced that student Harwan Anyaube is dealing drugs in the high school. After many attempts, Mr. Alexander convinces the superintendent to bring in an undercover agent to pretend to be a student and to catch Harwan. The agent is secured, and six months later, seven arrests are made. Harwan is among those expelled for dealing drugs. Although the agent's final report does not mention individual teachers, members of the faculty file a grievance through their union against the security agent, because they are incensed that another adult was in their classrooms without their knowledge, and they believe he could have been evaluating their teaching performance.

Main Topic

Police in schools

Subtopics

School climate and atmosphere

Substance abuse

Unions

Decision making

Possible Solutions

Mr. Alexander should

1. Ask a reporter to write a story about the union's actions.

2. Respond to the grievance in a very insulting manner to show how silly the grievance is.

3. Ignore the grievance, because eliminating the dealers from the school population is what really counts.

4. Ask to meet with the union president to explain the decision to bring the undercover agent into the school, and promise to include union representatives in the decision-making process if a similar situation occurs.

What Would You Do?

_____

_____

_____

_____

_____

What Really Happened

Mr. Alexander spoke with several union leaders about the issue. The union only wanted to be on record in case accusations were made in the future about the performance of teachers who had an agent in their classes. The grievance was dropped when the administration offered to place a letter, which described the events, in the file of each teacher who had had the undercover agent in class.

What Should Have Happened and Why

This action took place long before challenges to such police involvement in schools became controversial and litigious. The administration had secured proper permission for the placement of the agent in the school, and drug dealers were removed from the school.

Most states now have a memorandum of agreement between law enforcement officials and boards of education that clearly outlines the responsibilities and circumstances that would bring law enforcement officials into the schools. These memoranda become policy and set standards of authority and behavior for all involved.

How Much Does an A in History Go for Now?

SNAPSHOT 4-6

Mr. Schnell, superintendent of Midvale Schools, is attending a community meeting when Mrs. Ramirez asks if 400 dollars is the going rate for an A in Mr. Rader's class. The superintendent turned pale and asked what she meant. Mrs. Ramirez explained that she had just moved to the United States from a South American country in which paying teachers for specific grades is a common practice. She had been giving her daughter 400 dollars a month for the last three months to give to Mr. Rader.

Main Topic

Rumors

Subtopic

Ethics

Possible Solutions

Mr. Schnell should

1. Send a substitute to call Mr. Rader to come to the meeting immediately.

2. Laugh at the accusation, because it is so ludicrous.

3. Bring Mrs. Ramirez and Mr. Rader together for a meeting as soon as possible.

4. Bring Mrs. Ramirez's daughter in for a conference.

What Would You Do?

_____

_____

_____

_____

_____

What Really Happened

Mrs. Ramirez and her daughter met with the superintendent and the teacher at noon that day. The student admitted that she was taking money from her parents and saying it was to bribe the teacher. She was using the money to buy clothes and for social-life expenses.

The superintendent sent an overnight letter to each parent who had attended the meeting; he explained that investigation had revealed the accusation as false. The rumor then died quickly.

What Should Have Happened and Why

Mr. Schnell did an excellent job demanding a meeting with the student and the parent as soon as possible. By resolving the issue and sending the letter to the parents who attended the meeting, he was able to reduce the damage that would certainly have been done to Mr. Rader's reputation.

Situations of this nature cannot be foreseen or anticipated. Teachers need to listen to and be aware of rumors and stories that can negatively affect their reputations or the reputations of their colleagues. Reacting quickly and decisively to a rumor usually prevents negative newspaper headlines and the destruction of a teaching career.

SNAPSHOT 4-7

"Make Sure You .gov, Not .com"

Seventh-grade social studies teacher John Torme is taken totally by surprise one afternoon when Mrs. Baker angrily enters his classroom screaming at the top of her lungs. She throws several sheets of paper at him, which depict a number of men and women performing sexual acts. Finally, she calms down enough to accuse him of forcing her daughter to do homework on her home computer that involved logging on to a pornographic Web site.

Main Topic

Lesson plans

Subtopics

Parental involvement

Civility in school

Possible Solutions

Mr. Torme should

1. Gather the papers, and walk out of the room before Mrs. Baker becomes more angry.

2. Request a meeting with the principal immediately.

3. Yell back at Mrs. Baker that he would never do such a thing.

4. Pull out his lesson plan, and show it to Mrs. Baker.

What Would You Do?

_____

_____

_____

_____

_____

What Really Happened

Mr. Torme had requested that students write a report on the White House, the presidential residence in Washington, DC. One of the references he had written on the assignment sheet for the students was thewhitehouse.gov. Mrs. Baker's daughter logged on to thewhitehouse.com, which is a pornographic site. She had not read the assignment sheet carefully and did not even know the .gov extension existed. Mrs. Baker did not believe Mr. Torme and filed a complaint against him, refusing to look at the site when he and the principal tried to show her the difference.

What Should Have Happened and Why

There was very little that Mr. Torme or the principal could do to calm Mrs. Baker down. Mr. Torme had submitted his lesson plans to the principal with the .gov Web site clearly designated. He was not, therefore, in violation of any district policy and was not disciplined by the district.

Mr. Torme had not known of the existence of the pornographic site. If the assignment had been done in school, the district filtering software would have denied entrance to the pornographic site. Because the

Bakers did not own or subscribe to a filtering service at home, their daughter's computer obeyed her command to enter the site.

The principal required all teachers to emphasize to their students the importance of copying Web site addresses exactly. The Bakers were spammed by other pornographic sites because their computer had logged on to the first site. They eventually bought a commercial filtering service for their home computer.

This is a lesson for all teachers and parents about the value of filtering services and software. In addition, all teachers should double-check Web sites and any reasonable variation, prior to placing a site on a student assignment sheet. The Internet can be both a wonderful resource and the most wicked creation of all time. Being able to use it appropriately becomes one of the most important of all lessons in school.

"Not My Kid"

Mrs. Hung, the advanced-placement physics teacher, attends a workshop on the values of cooperative learning and decides to implement the concept in her class. She divides students into four groups, assigning them to specific groups on the basis of performance and aptitude. All goes well until Dr. Richards sends her a letter demanding that his daughter not participate in the experience, because she is "doing the teacher's job by instructing the less able students in the class and so is not progressing at the rate she should."

Main Topic

Teaching style

Subtopic

Parental involvement

Possible Solutions

Mrs. Hung should

1. Continue using the cooperative method, because she is the teacher.

2. Request a meeting with Dr. Richards to discuss the methodology.

3. Give the letter to the principal, and let him settle the issue.

4. Send a copy of the literature from the workshop she attended to Dr. Richards to read.

What Would You Do?

_____

_____

_____

_____

_____

What Really Happened

Mrs. Hung requested a meeting with Dr. Richards, during which she discussed the value of cooperative learning and offered to make his daughter the lead student. Based on information she found in a progressive teaching guide to developing thinking skills, *Taxonomy of Educational Objectives* (Bloom et al., 1956), Mrs. Hung was able to convince Dr. Richards that his daughter would learn more and retain more by teaching the subject matter to other students in the class. She could tell him that through cooperative learning, his daughter would evaluate the material in ways that increased her immersion and involvement. By understanding and internalizing the material and then explaining it in her own words so other students could understand it, she would become more knowledgeable herself. Dr. Richards was satisfied and accepted the offer of a leadership position for his daughter.

What Should Have Happened and Why

Mrs. Hung did a great job providing the appropriate information for Dr. Richards in a very professional way.

References

Bloom, B., et al. (Eds.). (1956). *Taxonomy of educational objectives: The classification of educational goals by a committee of college & university examiners.* New York: Longmans, Green.

Brophy, J. (2000). *Teaching.* Philadelphia: Temple University Center for Research in Human Development & Education.

Canter, L., & Hausner, L. (1987). *Homework without tears.* New York: Harper & Row.

5

Complying With School Policy and Legal Requirements

"Don't You Dare Tell Anyone"

One evening Miss Oliveri stayed late in school to complete some copying on the big copier in the teachers' workroom. The copier ran out of toner, and Miss Oliveri went to the storeroom to get a new packet. As she entered the storeroom, she found a young male custodian and a female special-education student in a compromising position. The custodian threatened her with bodily harm if she told anyone what she had seen.

Main Topic

Child abuse

Subtopics

Sexual behavior

Threats

Possible Solutions

Miss Oliveri should

1. Call the police immediately.

2. Report the incident to the administration.

3. Call the parents of the female student.

4. Do nothing, because the custodian may physically harm her.

What Would You Do?

_____

_____

_____

_____

_____

What Really Happened

Miss Oliveri reported the incident and the threat to the police and to the administration. After interviewing the girl, the police arrested the custodian and charged him with statutory rape. He was released from his position as a custodian. As a result of a plea bargain, the charges were reduced to inappropriate sexual contact, and the custodian was sentenced to two years in county jail and fined $5,000.

What Should Have Happened and Why

Miss Oliveri was correct to call the police and report the incident to the administration. Teachers need to place the safety and well-being of students above all else and to depend on the authorities to do their jobs.

The emotional stress caused by such incidents can produce crises of professional choice. Teachers must be prepared to understand that such threats can come from any direction at any time and when least expected. Although there have been a number of violent incidents reported by the media about students, threats and acts of violence can be perpetrated by anyone.

New teachers need to research and reflect on the possible dangers that can invade their workplace. School districts must develop policies for such possibilities, and teachers must become totally aware of their responsibilities under such policies. The major lesson of Columbine must be a heightened awareness that anyone who hears threats from students or others must take them seriously and report the threats immediately to the authorities.

A positive working relationship between schools and the police is crucial. All teachers need to follow the directions given by the professionals in this arena, just as they would expect others to respect their professional advice when it comes to educational matters. Many people will continue to believe that nothing of this nature will happen in their school. These NIMBYs (Not in My Back Yard) are deluding themselves. The possibility is everywhere, and the only way to combat it is to be prepared.

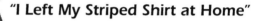

"I Left My Striped Shirt at Home"

SNAPSHOT 5-2

During an after-school parent conference about Joey's progress in Mr. Blake's class, Joey and his father, Mr. Donrem, argue loudly. Mr. Donrem stands up, slaps Joey across the face, rips his shirt, and slams him with his shoulder.

Main Topic

Child abuse

Subtopics

Parental reaction

Violence in school

Possible Solutions

Mr. Blake should

1. Try to get between father and son to prevent further contact.

2. Leave the room to remove himself from possible harm, and call for an administrator.

3. Call the police.

4. Try to counsel Mr. Donrem and Joey.

What Would You Do?

_____

_____

_____

_____

_____

What Really Happened

Mr. Blake stepped between the parent and the student and prevented further contact between them. There was a great deal of tension, but Mr. Donrem calmed down and apologized for losing his temper.

After the father and child left the school, Mr. Blake reported the father to the youth authorities for striking his son. An investigation revealed that Joey was the victim of ongoing child abuse. He was sent to live with his mother, who had divorced Mr. Donrem several years ago. Although he now lived in another town, school authorities gave him permission to finish out the school year in his present school.

What Should Have Happened and Why

Mr. Blake was wise to call the police immediately to prevent further violence and to place the incident on record. In doing so, he protected himself and the school district from legal liability. He was a witness to an assault that occurred on school property.

Teachers need a working knowledge of school law as it relates to the actions of parents and possible physical abuse. If a district does not offer such information, the teacher must obtain preventative information from other sources including, but not limited to, the teachers' association or union.

SNAPSHOT 5-3

Body Language

During a parent conference with Miss Shoe-maker, Mr. Binions mentions that he doesn't take any crud from his son, Kevin. If Kevin screws up in school he knows he won't sit down for a week. Miss Shoemaker remembers that Kevin was very uncomfortable in class the day after she returned to him a test that he had failed. Mr. Binions mentions in the course of the conversation that he likes to keep his family business private.

Main Topic

Child abuse

Subtopic

Threats

Possible Solutions

Miss Shoemaker should

1. Report the threat to the administration.

2. Contact the police immediately after the conference.

3. Contact the division of child abuse immediately.

4. Dismiss the conversation as just talk.

What Would You Do?

_____

_____

_____

_____

_____

What Really Happened

Miss Shoemaker reported the incident to Kevin's guidance counselor, who met with all of Kevin's teachers and the vice-principal. They agreed that all of them would keep an eye on Kevin and report any future signs of overt abuse to the youth authorities. Without further incident, Kevin graduated with his class.

What Should Have Happened and Why

Although Miss Shoemaker reported the incident to the guidance counselor, who in turn reported it to the division of child abuse, she should have also reported it directly to the administration. By doing so, she would have placed the incident on record and have gained support for herself and the counselor. It is the teacher's responsibility to make sure the administration is aware of such matters.

Most districts have a chain of command and standard operating procedures. Teachers need to become familiar with these hierarchies and procedures and to respect and follow them. Should an incident ever lead to litigation, the policies and procedures of the district and how the employees behaved will be at issue. A breakdown in these areas or in the chain of command can damage the district's case.

All teachers need to have a working knowledge of the dos and don'ts for identifying and reporting abuse.

"One More F and I'll . . . "

SNAPSHOT 5-4

Mr. Havlin hands back a set of tests to his class and asks that James stay after class to speak to him about his performance. Before they can speak to each other, James's best friend, Andrew, takes Mr. Havlin aside and tells him that James's father beats him when he brings home failing grades.

Main Topic

Child abuse

Subtopics

Rumors

Trust

Possible Solutions

Mr. Havlin should

1. Believe the story, and give James a passing grade.
2. Report the possible child abuse to the administration and to the child abuse authorities.
3. Report the possible child abuse to the guidance department.
4. Talk to James privately, and ask if it is true that his father beats him.

What Would You Do?

_____

_____

_____

_____

_____

What Really Happened

Mr. Havlin reported the incident to the administration and to the child abuse authorities. When an administrator called James's dad, the dad calmly asked if he could meet with the teacher and the principal. During the meeting, he mentioned that James had been playing games with him lately and that he wasn't sure he could trust his son. Andrew eventually admitted to his counselor that James had put him up to making the statements to the teacher, hoping the teacher would give him a passing grade out of sympathy. James's dad apologized for his son to the teacher and James's academic effort improved dramatically.

What Should Have Happened and Why

Teachers must be leery of such excuses. They should use the guidance department and other teachers to gather information about students.

Students can be very creative in the ways that they test teachers. Teachers need to develop a caring demeanor and learn to listen without making an immediate commitment to students. However, they cannot fall for every story a student presents. A teacher who is not taken in earns the respect of the entire educational community and will eventually be able to help students who have real issues and problems.

This is one aspect of the job that separates teachers from master teachers. The respect and reputation a teacher earns are worth much more than can be imagined.

"Not Me!"

SNAPSHOT 5-5

Mr. Gimas, a teacher, barges into Principal Honers's office with George Wrenner in tow. Mr. Gimas accuses George of smoking in the men's room, because there was a cigarette butt in the urinal in front of which George was standing. The school had just installed automatic flushers, so George must have been smoking, because he was still standing in front of the urinal. George vehemently denies smoking, and Mr. Gimas says he did not see smoke come out of George's mouth. How can George prove his innocence or at least establish reasonable doubt?

Main Topic

Due process

Subtopic

Reasonable suspicion

Possible Solutions

Mr. Honer should

1. Recognize that Mr. Gimas must be right, and suspend George for smoking.
2. Give George an opportunity to demonstrate how the butt could have been placed in the urinal.
3. Ask to see if George has any other cigarettes of the same brand in his pockets.
4. Call George's parents to have them present when George empties his pockets.

What Would You Do?

_____

_____

_____

_____

_____

What Really Happened

George was able to demonstrate that if someone throws a butt into the urinal and then stands in front of the urinal, the butt remains there until the person moves away, and the automatic flusher operates. Mr. Gimas was quite angry that George was not suspended. (See follow-up snapshot 7-5.)

What Should Have Happened and Why

Teachers must personally view a transgression before bringing disciplinary charges against a student. Students do not leave their rights as citizens at the front door of the school. Teachers and school staff members have a responsibility to treat students appropriately, because the lessons learned in the informal curriculum will be transferred to the outside world by the students, who relate authority to school personnel.

In this case, Mr. Gimas did not understand two basic premises of our society: that a person is considered innocent until proven guilty and that reasonable doubt is cause to dismiss a charge. It is better that 10 guilty parties go free than that 1 innocent party be falsely condemned.

SNAPSHOT 5-6

The Electronic Cheat Sheet

While giving a test, Mr. Cline notices that Eddie's collar is up. He has a small, single earphone in his ear.

Main Topic

Search and seizure

Subtopics

Cheating

Parental reaction

Trust

Possible Solutions

Mr. Cline should

1. Rip the earphone out of Eddie's ear and demand an explanation.

2. Let Eddie finish the test, and confront him as he is leaving the classroom, so as not to embarrass him in front of his classmates.

3. Report the incident to the vice-principal.

4. Do nothing, because he cannot prove the earphone is being used
to cheat.

What Would You Do?

_____

_____

_____

_____

_____

What Really Happened

Eddie was accused of cheating. He refused to empty his pockets
until his parents came to school. His father is a lawyer. On advice from
his dad, Eddie turned the microrecorder over to the principal. The tape
contained sections of the textbook. Eddie had not even tried to con-
dense the material. He was assigned an F on the test and suspended in-
school for 3 days.

What Should Have Happened and Why

Mr. Cline was quite astute to notice the hidden earphone. Students
have discovered different and ingenious ways to cheat. In many cases,
if students would put the effort into studying for tests that they put into
cheating, they would not need to cheat. Teachers can reduce the inci-
dence of cheating by being vigilant during testing situations. Moving
around the room, checking papers while students are working, noticing roving eyes, checking desks for Post-it notes stuck underneath the
tops, checking desktops for crib notes written right on the desk, checking see-through pens for crib notes, checking pencils for crib notes written right on the pencil, noticing writing on body parts, looking for open
notebooks on the floor, checking for watches that have calculator and
translation capabilities, clearing calculators that have programmed for-

mulas, printing tests on paper of different colors, developing different forms of the same test, rearranging the order of the questions, and other strategies help teachers catch cheats.

Teachers can go a long way toward preventing cheating by providing students with the proper preparation for the test. Test what is taught, encourage study groups, teach students proper test-taking techniques, provide review papers, and offer extra help. Students will generally not cheat if they understand the teacher's expectations and if tests are fair, represent the material taught, and are graded appropriately. Effective teachers do not need to become policemen during testing. Students respect teachers who make it known to their students that testing is considered a very important component of the class routine and that students are only cheating themselves when they cheat on a test.

The effective teacher will follow up suspected incidents of cheating and implement the school district policy when necessary. The effective teacher also uses the test as a teaching tool and not for the sole purpose of evaluation. By requiring students to correct their mistakes and offering retests for extra credit or completion points, teachers give students an opportunity to analyze mistakes—a higher level thinking skill. Teachers should be very concerned when students look at a graded test, crumple it up, and dump it in the wastebasket without trying to ascertain why they were not successful.

Unfortunately, a tremendous amount of pressure is placed on students to cheat. Grades have become the paramount issue for many parents, and pressure to get into the *right* college leads to high test-anxiety. High school students today are required to receive 35% more credits to receive a high school diploma than their parents were. Standards to remain eligible for interscholastic athletics and for acceptance into Division One athletic programs have increased dramatically over the last 15 years, especially with the creation of the National Collegiate Athletic Association (NCAA) Clearing House. NCAA rules call for students to have both a minimal academic record and SAT scores to be considered for Division One schools (for example, Notre Dame, Pennsylvania State, Ohio State). The clearinghouse acts as a filter for students who apply to these schools, to make sure their academics are high enough. The competition is tough. To top it all, the modern student culture accepts or condones cheating. Teachers have a difficult issue to wrestle with here.

Did She or Didn't She?

Mrs. Martin, a school counselor, is walking past a water fountain at which she sees Joan Hale put something small in her mouth, take a drink of water, and throw her head back, swallowing.

Main Topic

Search and seizure

Subtopics

Substance abuse
Student rights
Policy
Parental reaction

Possible Solutions

Mrs. Martin should

1. Confront Joan, and search her pocketbook to see if there are any other pills in her possession.
2. Report the incident to the administration immediately.
3. Ask Joan if she is feeling well, and counsel her about taking medication in school.
4. Call 911 to have an ambulance pick Joan up and to have her stomach pumped at the hospital.

What Would You Do?

_____

_____

_____

_____

_____

What Really Happened

This student was suspended pending a blood test. The test came back negative, and the student returned to class within two days. The teacher was considered to be "save harmless" under the circumstances.

What Should Have Happened and Why

Mrs. Martin followed the district policy related to substance abuse. But as a counselor, she was in a precarious situation. She needed to acquire the trust of students to come to her with their problems, including issues of substance abuse. This was a real dilemma for her. However, this was not a case in which Joan approached Mrs. Martin, so confidentiality was not required. The policy of the district calls for all medications to be on file with the school nurse and to be ingested only in the nurse's office under the supervision of the nurse. Not knowing what a student is taking can be dangerous to the individual student and to other students as well. All professionals in the school setting need to enforce such policies.

Party Time

SNAPSHOT 5-8

On a Friday afternoon, teachers are dismissing students for the weekend. Mr. Nort is standing in his classroom doorway when he overhears a conversation among students, who are saying that Mr. and Mrs. Warrington are away for the weekend and there is going to be a party at their house. The students whom he overhears are planning to crash the party and take alcohol and drugs.

Main Topic

Substance abuse

Subtopics

Teacher responsibility

Extension of school authority

Possible Solutions

Mr. Nort should

1. Call the police, and report the possible illegal party.

2. Try to contact Mr. Warrington to warn him.

3. Report the conversation to the administration.

4. Call the parents of the students who plan to crash the party.

What Would You Do?

_____

_____

_____

_____

_____

What Really Happened

Mr. Nort and the assistant principal called Mr. Warrington and the police to report the planned party. Mr. Warrington's brother went to the house that night, and the police caught the students with the controlled substances when they arrived. Mr. Warrington was very grateful and offered Mr. Nort a reward. Mr. Nort refused the reward, because he was simply doing his job. The arrested students were charged with possession and were remanded to municipal court, because no school rules were broken.

What Should Have Happened and Why

School personnel in the hallways during dismissal can hear amazing things. Students have no expectation of privacy in the common areas of the school. A quality working relationship with the local police department is critical to keep this type of information flowing to the authorities. As long as police are willing and able to maintain confidentiality about their source for such information, illegal student behavior can be partially curtailed.

"If It Walks Like a Duck"

SNAPSHOT 5-9

Mr. Nast is a young teacher who enters the men's room and observes Randy Conklin slide what appears to be a sandwich bag full of a green substance down the front of his jeans.

Mr. Nast was involved in a drug bust a year ago when Randy was found to be in possession of a controlled substance. Randy's dad promised to "get" Mr. Nast someday. Mr. Nast takes Randy to the vice-principal's office and, after some discussion, Randy takes out the bag and gives it to the vice-principal, Mr. Torres. Mr. Torres suspends Randy and calls his father.

Main Topic

Substance abuse

Subtopics

Search and seizure

Due process

Possible Solutions

Mr. Nast should

1. Request that the substance be tested before any charges are leveled against Randy.

2. Feel good about himself, because he caught Randy again, proving his actions last year were solid.

3. Contact the union lawyer to put him on alert.

4. Call the police to report the threat from last year and the circumstances of today.

What Would You Do?

_____

_____

_____

_____

_____

What Really Happened

Mr. Nast was correct to be wary. Randy's father had instructed his son to "get caught" with a bag of oregano and parsley, thinking the school would just assume that what the bag contained was marijuana. He would then have reason to seek Mr. Nast's removal. Randy was suspended anyway under the "look alike" law in the state.

What Should Have Happened and Why

Teachers and other school personnel must be prepared to follow all steps to ensure an appropriate search and seizure of controlled, dangerous substances. In many cases, the actions of the school personnel will be on trial more than those of the student. Most school district policies have a timeline and chain-of-custody form that records the actions of all the personnel in the situation. To show a breakdown in the policy, most defense lawyers will focus on the procedures followed by the school employees, thus creating a loophole that gets the charges dismissed. All teachers need to receive staff-development training to ensure consistent application of the district policies in such situations. Failure to know the procedures is not an excuse.

Thou Shalt Not Rat on Thy Fellow . . .

SNAPSHOT 5-10

The principal asks Mr. Macon to substitute for a fellow teacher who is attending a meeting that has gone beyond its scheduled time.

Mr. Macon begins to look for something to do with the class, and he opens the bottom desk drawer and finds a half empty bottle of vodka under some papers.

Main Topic

Substance abuse

Subtopics

Staff impropriety

Teacher responsibility

Possible Solutions

Mr. Macon should

1. Take the bottle, and dispose of it off school property to protect his fellow teacher.

2. Hide the bottle, and tell the other teacher that he is aware of the bottle and that he needs to get rid of it.

3. Report the incident to the administration immediately.

4. Ask the president of the union to help.

What would you do?

_____

_____

_____

_____

_____

What Really Happened

Mr. Macon went to the union president, and the union offered help to the teacher. After much denial, the teacher admitted to drinking on the job but never in front of students. He was given medical leave, and he returned to his duties six months later.

What Should Have Happened and Why

The administration should have been involved in this situation. Although confidentiality was in place, and the union was able to talk the teacher into seeking help, the fact that the liquor was on school property violated district policy, state law, and the union contract. It would be a public-relations nightmare should the facts of this case become public, because it resembles a cover-up on the part of the administration and the union. This is the type of situation that makes headlines.

Got the Munchies?

A student has been arriving late in Mr. Sidman's first-period class for the past two weeks. He has an air of apathy, has been eating his lunch at his desk during class, wears his outside coat in class, and has a strange stale odor.

Main Topic

Substance abuse

Subtopics

Due process

Search and seizure

Possible Solutions

Mr. Sidman should

1. Follow the student from his home to see if he is buying pot on the way to school.

2. Report his suspicions to the administration.

3. Report his suspicions to the school nurse.

4. Report his suspicions to the student's counselor.

What Would You Do?

_____

_____

_____

_____

_____

What Really Happened

Mr. Sidman reported his observations to the guidance department. During a meeting with the student's parents, counseling was offered. The student attended the counseling sessions with his parents, changed his circle of friends, and graduated with his class without any further incident.

What Should Have Happened and Why

This is a case of an astute teacher recognizing the overt signs of marijuana use and using the resources of the school district to find help for the student. All teachers need to recognize such signs and be familiar enough with the help available to students and families to ensure that the problems can be addressed.

Overt signs of marijuana use include rapid change of friends, the munchies, lethargic attitude, possession of drugs, a drop in grades and effort, odor of drugs, or cover-ups (such as the use of incense), conversation about drugs, hostility when discussing drug use, slogans on clothing and jewelry, political involvement to legalize drugs, uncleanliness, and so forth. An excellent Web site for more information is thefunplace.com/guild/indicators.html.

"Holding—15 Yard Penalty"

SNAPSHOT 5-12

Mr. Orbison, a teacher, is attending a football game on a Friday night at the high school where he teaches. He is there as a spectator, not as a chaperone. But he notices several students going to an automobile every 15 minutes. The students are quite boisterous. He decides to follow them to the car and finds several empty beer cans on the ground near the trunk of the car.

Main Topic

Substance abuse

Subtopics

Due process

Teacher responsibility

Possible Solutions

Mr. Orbison should

1. Call the police to come search the car.
2. Because he is not an official chaperone, he really can't do anything.
3. Report the evidence to the administrator in charge.

4. Ask a passerby to send an official to the car, because he cannot allow the students to drive away if they have been drinking.

What Would You Do?

_____

_____

_____

_____

_____

What Really Happened

The students were using the car as a large cooler for beer. The spare-tire wheel well was lined with heavy plastic, and ice and beer were placed on top. The vice-principal used the evidence of empty cans as cause for a school administrator to search the car. The students were suspended and provided with counseling. The teacher was praised for his observation and for reporting the incident.

What Should Have Happened and Why

Teachers and administrators should report in writing any suspicion of alcohol or substance abuse to the administration as soon as possible. Collect any evidence and secure the area if warranted.

Whether the teacher is an official chaperone for the event taking place is irrelevant. Authority of school personnel is in place on school property at all times. In this case, reasonable suspicion was present, and the district did not need to have probable cause to search the car. School officials only need to meet the requirement of reasonable suspicion if the car is on school property.

Mr. Orbison would have been derelict in his duty had he allowed the students to leave in the car if they were inebriated. Had the students then become involved in an accident, he could have been held liable, because he suspected the alcohol and failed to act. This is a real burden on teachers that must be understood.

Born to Be Wild

A student in Miss Anderson's class jumps on top of a desk and begins to play the air guitar, singing loudly. Several students try to calm him down. He becomes hostile. He does not want to be touched. Several students shout that he has taken PCP (phencyclidine).

Main Topic

Substance abuse

Subtopics

Safety

Teacher responsibility

Search and seizure

Possible Solutions

Miss Anderson should

1. Tackle the student, and beat him over the head with the guitar.

2. Order all the other students out of the room, and use the intercom to call for an administrator.

3. Search the student's knapsack for evidence of PCP.

4. Ask several of the larger male students to grab the student to calm him down and carry him to the office.

What Would You Do?

_____

_____

_____

_____

_____

What Really Happened

The students were playing a game to get out of class. The air-guitar player was tested for substance abuse, and the results were negative. The entire class was assigned detentions, as if they had cut a class. The guitar player and the student who made the comment about PCP were suspended. One of the parents who claimed her child had not taken part in the "conspiracy" appealed to the board of education, and the appeal was denied. No further appeals came forth.

What Should Have Happened and Why

Teachers need to treat any suspicion of substance abuse as the real thing. Suspecting that the students were trying to disrupt the class or prevent it from taking place would not have been proper procedure.

Teachers also need to know the behavior that indicates substance abuse and the slang terms used in the community to identify drugs and combinations of drugs. Regular in-service visits from the police or health care professionals during faculty meetings—to share information about the terms used, the types of drugs prevalent in the community, and typical behavior of those using drugs—are among the best methods a district can use to keep the faculty up-to-date.

This incident was a conspiracy to avoid class that backfired on the main players in the class.

"Ouch"

Mr. Ragan is a physical education teacher. Jennifer is hit in the abdomen by a soccer ball and collapses on the field. She is pregnant but is not aware of this yet.

Main Topic

Tort liability

Subtopics

Crisis management

Safety

Possible Solutions

Mr. Ragan should

1. Send a student immediately to get the school nurse.

2. Move Jennifer off the field so the class can continue.

3. Move students away from Jennifer, and refuse to move her until proper medical help arrives.

4. Call Jennifer a wuss, and get her back in the game—her team is down by only one goal.

What Would You Do?

_____

_____

_____

_____

_____

What Really Happened

Luckily, the teacher did not move Jennifer until the paramedics arrived. After the emergency squad took her to the hospital, tests revealed that Jennifer was pregnant. Her parents found out about her condition as a result of this event. Neither Jennifer nor the fetus was harmed by the incident.

What Should Have Happened and Why

Teachers must be prepared to obtain the help of the school nurse immediately. Do not move the student until the nurse or paramedics arrive. The teacher cannot be expected to be completely aware of a student's medical condition or history but can know the facts on file in the health office. Teachers should periodically check with the school nurse to update their knowledge.

In this case, Jennifer's parents were not aware of her condition. Teachers need to consider the worst-case scenario, when dealing with students who are injured, and take the appropriate actions to protect the student's physical well-being. Not knowing about a condition is not an excuse if the teacher is considered liable for taking actions that exacerbate the injury to a student.

The Butt Pincher

SNAPSHOT 5-15

Mr. Hartel was having a particularly bad day. He had a very persistent headache and cough. When he entered his classroom to teach his third-period class, Jimmy Houston was sitting in Mr. Hartel's chair. Mr. Hartel ordered Jimmy to sit in his own seat, but Jimmy did not move quickly enough for Mr. Hartel. To speed the process up, Mr. Hartel pinched Jimmy on the buttocks. Jimmy reacted by yelling at the teacher and running out of the classroom.

Main Topic

Tort liability

Subtopics

Child abuse

Classroom management

Possible solutions

Mr. Hartel should

1. Leave the class to follow Jimmy, and bring him back into the room.

2. Report the incident to the principal immediately, with an explanation that Jimmy was being disruptive and should be suspended.

3. Stay with the class, and find Jimmy as soon as possible to apologize for his indiscretion.

4. Call the union legal-aid office as soon as possible; he has a *big* problem.

What Would You Do?

_____

_____

_____

_____

_____

What Really Happened

The principal recognized the potentially explosive nature of the situation and immediately contacted the institutional-abuse section of the Division of Youth and Family Services. They, in turn, investigated the situation. Jimmy's parents contacted the state police to report an assault on their child. The parents met with the board of education. The board ordered that a letter be placed in Mr. Hartel's file detailing his lack of judgment and noting that he was never again to have any physical contact with a student.

The parents of the student filed a lawsuit naming the board of education, the administration, and the teacher as defendants. The suit claims their son was the victim of an abusive act and received "major psychological damage and trauma." The suit has not been tried yet.

Although the Division of Youth and Family Services and the state police have cleared the teacher of any criminal activity, the parents are persisting with the suit. The teacher and the administration have filed a countersuit for defamation of character and malice.

What Should Have Happened and Why

The principal was correct in reporting the incident to the state agency immediately. By doing so, he prevented even the hint of a cover-up or of inaction on the part of the district. Although the contract with the teachers' association called for the parents to meet with the teacher to resolve any complaints at the lowest level, state law superseded the contract.

Teachers must *never* touch a student under any circumstances unless the student is posing a danger to himself, other students, the teacher, or the property of others.

A reputation of this nature can destroy teachers within the community and make them totally ineffective. The psychological effects and stress of always being doubted by parents and students can be enormous. And if parents are concerned about the well-being and safety of their children in the school, teachers may not be able to complete their duties effectively.

Amazingly, a seemingly innocent action can take on the immense proportions of a case of this nature. Teachers must be aware that we live in a very litigious society that views school districts as entities with deep pockets. Many assume that school-district insurance companies will settle out of court instead of going to trial. This situation, which happened in less than two seconds, will be litigated for two to three years.

6 Responding to Perennially Sticky Issues

"Just When Do You Plan to Start Your Family?"

During her interview for her first teaching position, Ms. Sheperd was asked by the principal, after he made a comment about her engagement ring, what her plans were regarding marriage and starting a family.

Main Topic

Harassment

Possible Solutions

Ms. Shepherd should

1. Immediately stand and leave the interview, making sure the secretary hears her comments about harassment.

2. Go along with the question, and answer in a very vague way.

3. Claim that she does not intend to have children ever.

4. Mention that she plans to obtain tenure, and then begin her family.

What Would You Do?

_____

_____

_____

_____

_____

What Really Happened

Ms. Shepherd decided that, because she was the only witness to the improper question, she would not make an issue about it. She eventually secured a position in a neighboring district and now has three children, tenure, and a successful teaching career.

What Should Have Happened and Why

Under similar circumstances, any teacher who is seeking a position must develop a working knowledge of interview techniques and the legalities of the interview process. Under federal mandate, all districts are required to develop policies and procedures to ensure equity in hiring practices. These mandates come from such sources as the fourteenth amendment to the U.S. Constitution, Titles VI and VII of the Civil Rights Act of 1964, Title IX of the Education Amendments of 1972, Section 504 of the Rehabilitation Act of 1973, the Americans With Disabilities Act of 1990, Individuals With Disabilities Education Act of 1997, and numerous case law decisions.

At issue with many prospective teachers is the dilemma one faces should an equity issue become an issue that gains enough notoriety to affect future employment. This is a personal decision that the individual directly involved needs to address. The law does protect a person under such circumstances from being blacklisted. However, proving that a person has been discriminated against in such situations is difficult.

In this snapshot, Ms. Shepherd was able to secure a position in another district. However, she could have brought a case against the principal who asked this illegal question. Again, proving it was asked would be difficult.

SNAPSHOT 6-2

Hazing, Crazy Days of Fall

As Ms. Franz enters her homeroom one morning, she notices that all the members of the football team have shaved their heads. Ricky Lowden is having a hard time breathing, and he appears to be disoriented. She asks him what is wrong, and he mumbles that he was forced to drink a fifth of vodka last night as part of the freshman initiation to the football team.

Main Topic

Harassment

Subtopics

Hazing

Substance abuse

Violence in school

Possible Solutions

Ms. Franz should

1. Get the coach to come to the classroom immediately.

2. Report the situation to the administration immediately.

3. Call the nurse to come pick Ricky up.

4. Wait until Ricky is more coherent, and then make a decision.

What Would You Do?

_____

_____

_____

_____

_____

What Really Happened

The members of the football team who were involved in the hazing were removed from the team and suspended from school for 10 days. One of the parents appealed the suspension, saying it was double jeopardy. The board of education heard the appeal and upheld the administration's decision. The parents did not appeal any further.

What Should Have Happened and Why

Hazing has garnered a great deal of publicity through the media in recent years due to the cruelty and, in extreme cases, the deaths of young people involved. Most school districts have developed policies and procedures to counter such behavior.

Teachers must be prepared to understand the dangers of hazing and the signals that students exhibit, especially the victims of the hazing activity. In many cases, the victims do not want to make an issue of the situation, because peer pressure to go along with the action is extremely powerful. However, hazing is a crime against the person and must be reported to the administration and law enforcement authorities in writing.

SNAPSHOT 6-3

"Yeah, They're a Buncha . . . "

During a seemingly innocent conversation in the teachers' workroom, a colleague refers to a group of students in a racial minority group in a very demeaning manner. No one else in the room seems to care that the racist comments were made. Ms. Kyoto is personally offended by the comments.

Main Topic

Racism

Subtopic

Staff impropriety

Possible Solutions

Ms. Kyoto should

1. Ignore the comments, because this type of prejudice cannot be changed.
2. Gripe among other members of the staff who would feel the same way she does, in hopes that the word will get back to the prejudiced teacher.
3. Report the comments to the administration.
4. Confront the offensive person the first time they are alone together.

What Would You Do?

_____

_____

_____

_____

_____

What Really Happened

Ms. Kyoto eventually confronted the foul-mouthed teacher. He told her to mind her own business and claimed he never said anything inappropriate in front of students. Eventually, several parents complained about the teacher, and he took an early retirement after some counseling from the administration.

What Should Have Happened and Why

Teachers must realize that the teaching profession is not immune to people with radical points of view. Although these opinions may be contrary to one's personal viewpoint, teachers have a right to think in their own way. The line must be drawn, however, if and when it affects students. The best advice a teacher can receive is to avoid contact with individuals who express themselves in negative ways.

Many schools have become newsworthy due to the banishment of certain books and other resources, which promote a specific viewpoint about the treatment of minority and religious groups, American history classes and in society in general. This kind of issue generally leads to a controversy that involves First Amendment rights and the real messages conveyed to students about discrimination. This is not a controversy that will be resolved easily.

To be caught up in such a controversy can be damaging to a teacher's standing in the school and can be very time-consuming. The best way to avoid such controversy is to use only texts and supplemental materials approved by the board of education and listed in the curriculum for the school. Moreover, many teachers do not understand the concept that, once lesson plans are submitted to the administration and are approved, teachers are off the hook, and the contents of the lessons become the responsibility of the administration.

Education about prejudice, genocide, and hate crimes promotes tolerance, understanding, empathy, and acceptance of different cultures. However, this is not the responsibility of the social studies teacher alone. All teachers across the curriculum need to understand that comments, actions, reactions to current events, and the selection of course material will portray an image of the teacher that will be interpreted by students and the community. Being branded a racist is one of the most difficult disadvantages a teacher can try to overcome. One comment or action can make that brand stick. Teachers need to set themselves apart from such behavior completely.

An excellent source for materials on this subject is *Prejudice Reduction and Hate Crimes Prevention: An Annotated Bibliography of Resources for Teachers and Administrators* (New Jersey State Department of Education, 1997).

"M...R...R...I...C...H...M...A... N...I...S...A..."

Miss Hamner is the sponsor of the high school yearbook. As the final copies arrive for distribution to the entire school and the community, she notices a vulgar reference to the principal in the first letters of each successive entry of the class will.

Main Topic

Civility in school

Subtopic

Teacher responsibility

Possible Solutions

Miss Hamner should

1. Do nothing—no one will notice it because it is so hard to find.

2. Take the yearbook to the principal immediately.

3. Call the editors together to find out who was responsible.

4. Blame the yearbook printer for letting the reference enter into print, and demand new books immediately.

What Would You Do?

_____

_____

_____

_____

_____

What Really Happened

Miss Hamner spoke to members of the editorial staff, who denied involvement in the prank. They said it was a coincidence. Miss Hamner also reported her discovery to the administration. So that students would not see the inappropriate statement in the future, they were offered an insert (which rearranged the offending lines so they did not spell anything) as soon as the yearbook company could provide inserts. Five students requested the inserts for their yearbooks, out of 680 books sold. Miss Hamner did not apply for the position of yearbook adviser the next year.

What Should Have Happened and Why

Miss Hamner was correct to take the yearbook to the administration. Students can find many different ways to express themselves negatively. As the sponsor of the yearbook, it was her responsibility to proofread it. Her decision to remove herself as the yearbook adviser was a shame because she worked well with students, and her intentions were to provide a memorable yearbook in a positive way.

All too often, a sponsorship of clubs or organizations becomes the tail that wags the dog. Miss Hamner's involvement with the yearbook had nothing to do with her abilities to educate the students in her classes. She spent an inordinate amount of time feeling stress over the yearbook and the prank. She found out several years later, during a class reunion, who the culprit was. By then, it was too late to do anything about it, and the school district lost a quality teacher as yearbook adviser, one who had cared enough to go well beyond the classroom.

Teachers should communicate with one another about the responsibilities, obligations, and expectations of school groups they sponsor. All too often, the history of sponsorship is oral, and new sponsors disappoint students and staff members when they do not perform the same way their predecessors did. One way around this is to encourage the administration and other sponsors to develop a handbook for sponsors within the district. Similar to a job description, this document records the traditions and other little-known aspects of a school activity.

" . . . You Stupid &$#@!%$%#"

Mr. Ramahd is a young, newly appointed teacher. After school one day, he passes the gym, where a regionally famous and respected basketball coach is berating his team. The epithets are flowing profusely and loudly. One student athlete is clearly crying as the others begin to join in with the coach to berate the young man.

SNAPSHOT 6-5

Main Topic

Civility in school

Subtopic

Teacher misconduct

Possible Solutions

Mr. Ramahd should

1. Report this behavior to the administration.

2. Offer to help the coach, so he can better understand this motivational approach.

3. Call the parent of the player who was in tears, and explain what he just witnessed.

4. Inform the athletic director.

What Would You Do?

_____

_____

_____

_____

_____

What Really Happened

The teacher reported his discovery to the principal, who made it a point to visit the coach every day. The coach's inappropriate behavior continued, and he was fired. No parents complained about the firing, and no parents came to the board of education meeting to defend the coach. The coach had also bullied the community—parents revealed after the firing that their children were fearful of the coach. Many parents would not permit their children to become a part of his program because of his abuse.

Mr. Ramahd had expressed his concern about how other members of the staff would react to his "ratting out" the coach. The principal recognized this as a potential problem for Mr. Ramahd, because the coach did have a number of friends on the faculty who would defend him. Mr. Ramahd was promised confidentiality, and the principal was true to his word. Mr. Ramahd's name was never connected to the incident.

What Should Have Happened and Why

Mr. Ramahd was correct in reporting this type of behavior to the administration. Although the coach may be able to win games and bring championships to the school, the price for such victories should not be verbal abuse of student athletes. The use of profanity by a teacher is defined as unprofessional conduct and is grounds for dismissal in at least 14 states (McCarthy & Cambron-McCabe, 1987).

References

McCarthy, M., & Cambron-McCabe, N. (1987) *Public school law: Teachers' and students' rights.* Newton MA: Allyn & Bacon.

New Jersey State Department of Education. (1997). *Prejudice reduction and hate crimes prevention: An annotated bibliography of resources for teachers and school administrators.* Trenton, NJ: Author.

The Teacher as Professional

7

"Wasn't Lenin an Original Beatle?"

SNAPSHOT 7-1

Steve Landis, a student in Mr. Goodman's honors history class, asked an interesting question after class one day. He asked why Mr. Goodman would teach, glorify, and praise the virtues of the free enterprise system when the teacher was a member of the socialistic public school system.

Main Topic

Choice of profession

Subtopic

Politics

Possible Solutions

Mr. Goodman should

1. Use the opportunity as a *teaching moment.*

2. Laugh at Steve and change the subject.

3. Try to convince Steve that the public education system is not socialistic.

4. Quit his position as a teacher and go into business with Steve.

What Would You Do?

_____

_____

_____

_____

_____

What Really Happened

Mr. Goodman and Steve were able to have an excellent discussion about Steve's comment. Steve wound up working for a major accounting firm, and Mr. Goodman still teaches. Both are very happy with their career selection.

What Should Have Happened and Why

During class, Mr. Goodman offered all the students his reasons for becoming a teacher without allowing his explanation to take a major portion of class time. Mr. Goodman should have defended his choice of profession without being too defensive. All teachers must feel comfortable in their selection of career. A solid working knowledge of educational philosophy is the foundation for such a choice.

People often challenge teachers about their career choice. Clearly, the general public views teachers as working a short year and a short day and as being overpaid and protected by tenure and as a drain on the public tax coffers. However, once a critic becomes more aware of the complications and full extent of a teacher's responsibilities, the critic usually backs off.

All teachers have a responsibility to educate the public about myriad issues that confront teachers daily. Having the critics read the snapshots that appear in this book will go a long way toward educating the public.

Recent research has focused on job satisfaction among teachers. Administrative support, parental involvement, student behavior, and teacher control over classroom procedures were significant variables in teacher job satisfaction. Teachers who are able to develop quality working relationships with administrators, parents, and students find their desire to remain in the profession enhanced. Many ways exist to develop these skills. Further research of this topic will reward teachers well.

"And Our Selection Is . . . "

SNAPSHOT 7.2

Miss Zimawe, a young African American teacher, volunteers to be a member of the teachers' association's scholarship committee. The association offers a $5,000 award at graduation to the student who is the best role model for younger students. The committee leans toward awarding the scholarship to Bill Martin, a white student who is a football hero and who is very popular with the community and the staff. During the summer months, before she became a member of the faculty, Miss Zimawe was a social worker in the community and is aware of Bill's arrest for drug possession with intent to distribute. Confidentiality binds her because Bill's records are sealed because he was a minor when he was arrested. The next person in line for the scholarship is an African American student.

Main Topic

Confidentiality

Subtopics

Racism

Substance abuse

Teacher responsibility

Possible Solutions

Miss Zimawe should

1. Keep quiet, because confidentiality is in place.

2. Break confidence, tell several members of the committee about the arrest, and let them stop the award from going to Bill.

3. Fight vigorously for her candidate, although it will be a losing battle.

4. Point out the racial aspects of the situation, and use the *race card* to fight for her candidate.

What Would You Do?

_____

_____

_____

_____

_____

What Really Happened

Miss Zimawe maintained her confidentiality. Bill received the award and went off to college. He dropped out in less than one year.

What Should Have Happened and Why

Miss Zimawe faced a real dilemma in this situation. Her professional training as a social worker won out as it should have. She may have lost the battle in this case, but by keeping her position on the scholarship committee and searching for quality candidates for the future, she will continue to serve the community in a valuable manner. Although her thoughts were private, the fact that Bill lasted less than a year in college made her feel vindicated.

"I Leave to My Best Friend . . . "

Mr. Liberi is an English teacher who has a course requirement that promises confidentiality about students' writing in their daily journals. In today's entry, John Williams writes that he is anticipating death by his own hand.

Main Topic

Confidentiality

Subtopics

Suicide threats

Trust

Guidance services

Possible Solutions

Mr. Liberi should

1. Find John, and talk to him about his journal entry.
2. Report the entry to John's guidance counselor, and let her do her job.
3. Report the entry to the administration.
4. Call John's parents immediately, and ask them to come to school.

What Would You Do?

_____

_____

_____

_____

_____

What Really Happened

Mr. Liberi went directly to John's counselor, who brought the resources of the district into the situation. John spent most of the afternoon waiting for transportation to the mental-health crisis center. During that time, he spoke *in tongues* to the vice-principal, who had been one of his former teachers. John was diagnosed with severe problems and was placed in a residential setting for three years, until he gained a high school diploma and went to college. The counseling staff and the administration praised Mr. Liberi publicly for his actions.

What Should Have Happened and Why

One of the most frightening events of any teacher's life is the death of a student, especially when the student commits suicide, and the teacher may have had some evidence that the student was troubled. Teachers need to develop a sixth sense about their students, their lives outside of school, family situations, peer interactions, sibling rivalries, possible abuse, and more.

Most school districts have developed policies that require professionals to react in a manner that will bring the resources of the district into action immediately during a crisis. Teachers need to be trained to identify the signs and behaviors associated with self-destruction and to act swiftly, without hesitation, to bring the help necessary to a troubled child. Many legal ramifications exist for teachers in such situations.

If your district does not provide a training opportunity, seek one yourself. A good start would be local or state mental health associations or professional organizations and literature.

SNAPSHOT 7-4

The End Result Is a Better Understanding of . . .

During back-to-school night, Mr. Basland, a parent, engages Mr. Sophom, a teacher, in a deep philosophical discussion in front of all the other parents. Mr. Sophom's understanding of district policy and the curriculum is in direct opposition to Mr. Basland's. Mr. Sophom heatedly debates Mr. Basland, and both men become quite animated. Their confrontation becomes the talk of the community.

Main Topic

Ethics

Subtopics

Parental involvement.

Teacher as public persona

Policy

Possible Solutions

Mr. Sophom should

1. Ignore Mr. Basland, and remind everyone that the purpose of back-to-school night is to explain the curriculum.

2. Invite Mr. Basland to come to class one day to debate educational issues with the class.

3. Attack Mr. Basland with his perceptions of school philosophy.

4. Move toward Mr. Basland, and quietly ask him to discuss such matters when the other parents have left the room.

What Would You Do?

_____

_____

_____

_____

_____

What Really Happened

Mr. Basland and Mr. Sophom had quite a lively debate in the cafeteria later that evening. They eventually accepted each other's points of view and became good friends.

What Should Have Happened and Why

Although this situation is quite healthy, and educational philosophy and policies are always open to discussion, the purpose of back-to-school night is to provide information to parents about the curriculum and routines of specific classes. Mr. Sophom should have refrained from a debate of this nature when it was not the purpose of the evening.

To prevent this type of confrontation, teachers should prepare for back-to-school night in much the same way they would prepare for a class. Provide parents with handouts describing classroom rules, homework expectations, attendance regulations, and more. Prepare the classroom to receive visitors as one would prepare for visitors at home. A neat, organized workstation says much about how the teacher will set an example for students. Put textbooks and other resources on display for parents. Samples of exemplary work that students have completed help parents visualize what is expected of their children. Be prepared in this manner, and postpone until another time the type of discussion that took place between Mr. Basland and Mr. Sophom. Sometimes a parent has a grudge to bear about the running of the district or school. An individual classroom is not the forum for such discussion. If parents ask teachers to comment on controversial matters or policy beyond their job description, teachers should refer the parent to the appropriate administrator.

"Which Country Do We Live in Again?"

SNAPSHOT 7-5

In snapshot 5-5, Principal Honers lets George off, because the student is able to establish that he may not have thrown the cigarette butt into the urinal. Afterward, Mr. Gimas, the teacher involved in the situation, becomes irate and yells at Mr. Honers, "I am tired of reasonable doubt getting kids out of suspensions in this school!"

Main Topic

Insubordination

Subtopic

Reasonable suspicion

Possible Solutions

Mr. Honers should

1. Calmly request that Mr. Gimas put his concerns in writing.

2. Ask Mr. Gimas to file a grievance through the union.

3. Explain to Mr. Gimas the concepts of due process and reasonable doubt.

4. Walk away from Mr. Gimas without comment.

What Would You Do?

_____

_____

_____

_____

_____

What Really Happened

Mr. Honers wrote a letter to Mr. Gimas reminding him that students have rights and that reasonable doubt is a major factor in protecting individual rights in American society. After a meeting with the union representatives, the administration placed the letter in Mr. Gimas's file for two years and then removed the letter.

What Should Have Happened and Why

Mr. Gimas and teachers like him fail to recognize the lessons that schools are teaching each and every day through the manner in which authorities treat students. The effective teacher recognizes and understands the rights of students and treats them as citizens. Teaching is not autocratic control of the classroom but rather the creation of an environment in which students and teachers facilitate one another in the process of learning (Wong, 1990). Teachers who fail to learn from students fail themselves.

Teachers are obligated to possess a working knowledge of students' rights and the limits of their own authority as teachers. Possessing a full working knowledge of the discipline code is the best way to avoid embarrassing situations. Is there a difference between a student smoking and a smoking situation? If not, such a differentiation needs to be established as part of the code.

"Are You Sure You Can't Get This by . . . "

Mr. Bozman, a nontenured teacher, is asked by the administration to provide home instruction for a student diagnosed as HIV positive.

Main Topic

Professional obligation

Subtopic

Personal safety

Possible Solutions

Mr. Bozman should

1. Contact the union to see if he must perform this duty.

2. Contact the health department to assess his risks.

3. Refuse to perform this duty on the basis of religious convictions.

4. Recognize the rights of the child to receive an education, and do the best job possible.

What Would You Do?

_____

_____

_____

_____

_____

What Really Happened

The administration and others eventually convinced Mr. Bozman that it was safe to provide home instruction for the student. He completed the assignment, and the student graduated with his class.

What Should Have Happened and Why

Today's society is replete with issues of health hazards—from communicable diseases to asbestos in the schools. Teachers must be prepared to research the dangers and myths of contagious diseases and health hazards and act accordingly. People with AIDS, for example, enjoy civil rights protection in connection with their illness. People with some other diseases, however, may be subject to quarantine by the health department to control the spread of the disease.

By now, districts should have policies in place about students who are diagnosed with communicable diseases. Teachers should also check with their professional associations for advice. Every teacher needs right-to-know training. Although many teachers look down on this training as a waste of time, they need to know and understand any and all dangers that are present in their workplace.

Working within the global community, all teachers need to be fully aware of the AIDS epidemic. A website to help develop knowledge in this area is www.silcom.com/~stopaids.

SNAPSHOT 7.1

"We'll Have a Good Time Anyway"

The state in which Mr. Burton teaches has a law that all teachers must attend the yearly teachers' convention. None of the teachers in his school plans to attend, and they laugh when the principal announces that proof of attendance is required this year.

Main Topic

Teacher responsibility

Subtopic

Professional obligation

Possible Solutions

Mr. Burton should

1. Go to the convention.
2. Ask the union president for advice.
3. Find another young teacher with whom to go to the convention.
4. Book a vacation weekend, and enjoy the time off.

What Would You Do?

_____

_____

_____

What Really Happened

Mr. Burton decided to go to the convention alone. On the convention floor, he met the young lady whom he eventually married. He was glad he went.

What Should Have Happened and Why

Just as peer pressure exists for students, it also exists for teachers. Following the crowd or being branded a *rate buster* by fellow teachers generally leads to hurt feelings and confusion for teachers who have a strong work ethic. Teachers with a strong work ethic gravitate to others who have the same approach to their profession. Teachers ought to select a peer group that is compatible with their personal feelings toward their position. These teachers are willing and able professionals who consider the children the major concern in their positions.

On the other hand, many teachers will do only the minimum required under their contracts. Any union will defend the lowest common denominator in the organization, and this includes the teaching profession. Those whose attitude can be described as "union mentality" should consider their choice of profession and ask questions about their attitude and willingness to do all they can for the children in their care.

Generally, this attitude will be documented in the observation and evaluation process. Teachers who are willing and able to do their jobs will be left alone to work with minimum interference from the administration. Those who are unwilling will be provided staff-development opportunities to develop lagging skills. These teachers need attitude adjustments and a regeneration of energy to bring to the classroom. Counselors should advise those who are unwilling and unable to make more than a minimum effort to leave the teaching profession—for the sake of the children and the sake of other teachers in the community. One cannot be burned out unless one has been on fire.

A Minor Mistake

Mr. Dakari is the assistant principal. Ms. Collon has marked Barbara Winters absent in homeroom incorrectly. Barbara is present in school. However, the automatic calling-system has called Barbara's home and reported her absent. Mr. and Mrs. Winters are in Mr. Dakari's office and are very upset. The mother is crying, the father is pounding his fist, and the grandfather, who came along, too, looks ill. Over the weekend, Barbara's boyfriend threatened to kill her because she broke up with him. They demand to speak **immediately** to the teacher who marked their daughter absent!

Main Topic

Teacher responsibility

Subtopics

Rumors

Threats

Possible Solutions

Mr. Dakari should

1. Send a substitute to cover Ms. Collon's class, and ask Ms. Collon to report to the office immediately.

2. Bring in a guidance counselor to address the threat made to Barbara.

3. Call the police to report the threat.

4. Apologize for the mistake, and promise it will never happen again.

What Would You Do?

_____

_____

_____

_____

_____

What Really Happened

Mr. Dakari kept the parents away from Ms. Collon until the end of the day, hoping they would calm down. They did not. After leaving the school, Mr. and Mrs. Winters contacted an attorney and brought suit against the teacher and the district for emotional distress. The case was settled out of court when the district adjusted the automatic calling system procedures to double-check students' absences prior to making any calls.

What Should Have Happened and Why

This type of mistake will haunt a teacher for a very long time. Taking roll is routine and is only one task among the hundreds that a teacher does each week without much concern. However, circumstances can set up a situation such as the one described above. Teachers need to develop a daily routine that has double checks incorporated into the routines.

Mr. and Mrs. Winters had cause to be alarmed because they believed that the threat made against their daughter was serious and that the boy who made the threat was capable of carrying it out. Anticipating such a situation is not possible, because teachers cannot be aware of every event in every student's household and neighborhood or even of all students' school lives. The parents brought a lawsuit as a way to vent their frustration over the entire situation, but they were not attacking the teacher personally.

Stories of people suing school districts for every conceivable reason bombard students and parents. Most of these lawsuits are considered nuisance suits and are either dismissed or settled out of court. But the threats and rumors that lawsuits bring are costly and time-consuming to school districts and teachers.

"And in This Corner . . . "

SNAPSHOT 7-9

Ms. DeFerari is a 115-pound teacher. She is walking through the hallway during passing time when she hears the cry "Fight! Fight!" coming from around the corner. She enters the hallway to find two large football players violently punching each other on the floor.

Main Topic

Teacher responsibility

Subtopics

Crisis management

Safety

Tort liability

Possible Solutions

Ms. DeFerari should

1. Get away from the physical danger, because she stands no chance of breaking up this fight.

2. Jump into the center of the fracas, and order the two boys to stop—they would never hit a female teacher.

3. Keep other students away from the danger, and send some students to get help.

4. Call 911 from her cell phone.

What Would You Do?

_____

_____

_____

_____

_____

What Really Happened

The teacher prudently recognized that she could have been seriously hurt. She kept other students away from the action and sent others to get help. By the time the vice-principal arrived with several male teachers, both boys were exhausted and went to the office quietly.

What Should Have Happened and Why

Teachers must be prepared to recognize when they are not expected to risk physical harm. The overriding concept is that teachers should act as any reasonable adult would in the same circumstances. However, teachers can use various methods to restrain students.

Staff-development programs should train teachers in the use of such methods. Because violence in schools is a major issue today, this type of staff development is crucial. Administrations need to inform staff members of emergency plans, coordinate efforts with the police, and practice for such events as an armed intruder in the building, students with weapons, bomb threats, and more. Lockdowns in which teachers are provided with instructions to protect their students in the event of violent intruders are now as necessary as fire drills. Districts also need to develop crisis-management teams that can take swift action under such circumstances and help students during the aftermath of such events. Districts must also have the physical capabilities to lock classrooms and doors and have communication systems that allow teachers to communicate with the outside world.

Among the Missing

Miss Guidens takes her high school history class to visit a historical site approximately 150 miles from the school. About halfway home, one of the students on the bus whispers in Miss Guidens's ear that Rich Andre is not on the bus. Miss Guidens laughs and gets up to take roll again. She had called roll before the bus left, and all students had responded. But now, sure enough, Rich is not present.

Main Topic

Teacher responsibility

Subtopic

Extension of school authority

Possible Solutions

Ms. Guidens should

1. Stop the bus, and call the site office to see if Rich is waiting there.

2. If Rich is there, go back and get him.

3. If Rich is there, call a limo service to bring him home at her expense.

4. Totally panic if Rich is not at the site office.

What Would You Do?

_____

_____

_____

_____

_____

What Really Happened

One of the other students had answered "here" when Miss Guidens took roll the first time. He thought it would be funny to leave Rich behind. Rich wound up hitchhiking home and was able to arrive before the school buses. The parents never complained. Miss Guidens was reprimanded severely by the administration, and a strong letter was placed in her file. Nothing similar has happened since.

What Should Have Happened and Why

Taking a field trip is one of the most educational and pleasant experiences a teacher can bring to students. On the other hand, the responsibility a teacher assumes on such trips is extremely high. While on such trips, teachers need to assign students to specific chaperones and have periodic roll calls to ensure student presence. Miss Guidens now takes roll on field trips as students are entering the bus, and she takes another head count before the bus leaves.

Teachers need to have a clear understanding of district policies related to field trips and follow them to the letter. Parent permission forms, attendance during the trip and on transportation systems, student behavior, educational value, and social interaction are all major issues related to field trips.

Handwriting on the Wall

A teacher, Mr. Mincher, is using the boy's lavatory one morning when he reads "There's a bomb in the science lab" scrawled on the partition.

Main Topic

Teacher responsibility

Subtopics

Threats

Violence in school

Possible Solutions

Mr. Mincher should

1. Ask the custodians if this message has been on the wall for a while.

2. Report his finding to the administration immediately.

3. Call the police immediately.

4. Ignore it, because this kind of junk is on every partition in every public rest room.

What Would You Do?

_____

_____

_____

_____

_____

What Really Happened

Mr. Mincher reported the graffiti to the administration. An administrator questioned the custodians, who said the words had been there for several days. The administrator ordered the custodial staff to report all such findings immediately to the principal. From then on, an administrator checked the lavatories each morning before school opened, looking for such comments, and teachers checked the lavatories between periods for any kind of threat. Thus the creation of "potty check," as the teachers lovingly nicknamed their new responsibility.

What Should Have Happened and Why

The first person, adult or student, who observed the writing should have reported it to the administration, and the administration should have followed state law and district policy about district responsibility for such threats. Everyone would evacuate the building immediately until after the police had searched the entire school. Photographs of the graffiti should be taken, and the administration should attempt to find out when the writing was done and who had access to the lavatory at that time.

Teachers should have a record of who leaves their classrooms, when and where they are going, and the alleged purpose for leaving. As difficult as it is, staff members should monitor access to any rooms where, as in lavatories, students may be present without adults.

Bomb threats are very expensive for school districts. Think in terms of the salaries paid to all employees, the loss to the cafeteria in spoiled food, and the resources of the district going unused during the time that police secure the building. Add to these factors the disruption in student learning, and the expense is great.

Visit this Web site to find more information about steps that schools can take to prevent and catch those who perpetrate bomb scares—Proactive School Security and Crisis Preparedness Strategies at www.schoolsecurity.org/training/school-security.html.

"Hut One, Hut Two"

SNAPSHOT 7-12

On July 15, Mr. Simkins signs his first teaching contract to teach English for the next school year at Redview High School. On August 15, he is offered a contract to teach and coach football at Harrington High School. He loves football and has always wanted to coach at Harrington, his alma mater.

Main Topic

Teacher responsibility

Subtopics

Choice of profession
Contractual obligation

Possible Solutions

Mr. Simkins should

1. Resign immediately, and take the job at Harrington.

2. Recognize his obligation to Redview, and turn down the offer from Harrington.

3. Contact an attorney to review his options.

4. Submit his 60-day notice to Redview, and hope Harrington can wait until September 15.

What Would You Do?

_____

_____

_____

_____

_____

What Really Happened

The superintendent of Redview, incensed when Mr. Simkins resigned his position on August 16, filed charges against the teacher with the State Department of Education and tried to have his certification revoked. The charges were dropped when another candidate accepted the position in Redview, and school was able to open with a full staff.

What Should Have Happened and Why

The superintendent had every right to be angry with Mr. Simkins. When teachers sign a contract to teach, they assume a legal obligation to provide the services as contracted. By belatedly pulling out of his contract, Mr. Simkins reduced the pool of available teachers from which Redview could select and left them in the difficult position of finding a teacher to begin almost immediately. Harrington, if it knew of Mr. Simkins's obligation to Redview, should not have even offered the position to him. Mr. Simkins clearly was not acting in a professional manner, although he was lucky enough to teach and coach for Harrington. He did risk his certificate, because there was an excellent chance that Redview's superintendent would have been successful in canceling Mr. Simkins's certification.

Sucker Punch

Mr. Moon is a high school teacher, and a student comments to him in private that Bill and Joe are going to stage a fight in the cafeteria at lunchtime. When Mr. Knock, another teacher, comes over to break up the fight, one of the students is going to "take him out."

Main Topic

Teacher responsibility

Subtopics

Safety

Rumors

Confidentiality

Possible Solutions

Mr. Moon should

1. Ask the student who has provided the confidential information if the student would talk Bill and Joe out of their plan.

2. Forget confidentiality, and tell the principal immediately.

3. Tell Mr. Knock, and arrange for several other male teachers to be in the cafeteria to retaliate if Bill and Joe start a fight.

4. Call Bill and Joe's parents, and ask them to be in the cafeteria today.

What Would You Do?

_____

_____

_____

_____

_____

What Really Happened

Bill and Joe were suspended for conspiracy to harm a member of the teaching staff. Teachers in the school became much more aware of the possible dangers of violence in the school. At about the same time, national media reported that several students had placed poison in a teacher's coffee mug. Bill and Joe's parents did not appeal.

What Should Have Happened and Why

Teachers must be prepared to report any such rumors to the administration in writing. In this day and age, because any such threats must be taken seriously, many districts have adopted zero-tolerance policies. Some districts have been severely criticized for overreacting to situations. However, due to the injuries and even deaths of students, a policy of such dimensions is necessary to protect school-district staff members and all students.

Classroom teachers need to reinforce this policy in their classrooms whenever an opportunity arises. Only through consistency and repetition does the message sink in for every student and parent. Districts need to advertise the policy through newsletters and handbooks and require parents to sign off on statements that say they are aware of the full dimensions and consequences of zero tolerance. One wonders where the critics of zero tolerance will be when a district becomes lax, and a student is injured or killed.

"Could You Move the Wedding to November?"

SNAPSHOT 7-14

Ms. Christensen, a first-year teacher, is scheduled to be a bridesmaid in her best friend's wedding during the last weekend in September. During a brief conversation, Mrs. Sapp, president of the PTA, tells Ms. Christensen that everyone is looking forward to seeing her at the community picnic that weekend. She goes on to say that the picnic is a tradition in the community and that all new teachers are introduced by the mayor and given the key to the city. The citizens who pay her salary would interpret her nonparticipation in this festivity as a serious snub to them. Until this point, no one had mentioned this obligation to Ms. Christensen.

Main Topic

Teacher as public persona

Subtopics

Extension of school authority

Parental reaction

Professional obligation

Possible Solutions

Ms. Christensen should

1. Ask her friend to postpone the wedding.

2. Graciously back out of being in the wedding party by citing job obligations.

3. Risk the snub, and go to the wedding anyway.

4. Go to the wedding after calling Mrs. Sapp in the morning to tell her she is ill.

What Would You Do?

_____

_____

_____

_____

_____

What Really Happened

Ms. Christensen attended the wedding in Philadelphia. No one ever asked her why she did not attend the community picnic. Her key to the city was delivered to the school without comment from the mayor. Her nonattendance did not produce any negative results.

What Should Have Happened and Why

If the PTA expected teachers to attend a community function, they were obligated to send a formal invitation far enough in advance to permit teachers to make arrangements. Ms. Christensen should have explained to Mrs. Sapp that she had a previous commitment and would not be able to attend the community picnic. Ms. Christensen cannot be held accountable for Mrs. Sapp's lack of social grace. This would be a no-win situation for Ms. Christensen, however, if Mrs. Sapp commented to members of the PTA and the community that Ms. Christensen was ungrateful for the honor they wished to bestow on her.

Judge Janey

Mrs. Wescott has asked Mr. Windom to appear with her on a popular courtroom television show, on which they would argue about the grade her daughter received from him. She wants to split the appearance money with Mr. Windom.

Main Topic

Teacher as public persona

Subtopics

Grading policies

Parental reaction

Possible Solutions

Mr. Windom should

1. Go on the show and have fun.

2. Check with the administration first to see if there are any policies that would prohibit such appearances.

3. Deny the request, because grades are serious, and going on the show would trivialize the grading system.

4. Deny the request, because Judge Janey does not have the authority to change school grades.

What Would You Do?

_____

_____

_____

_____

_____

What Really Happened

After consultation with the administration and the union, Mr. Windom rejected the offer to appear on the television show. The grade was not changed.

What Should Have Happened and Why

Teachers must be prepared to place the integrity of the school district above sensational activities. Grading and evaluation of students is not a game and should not be open to any type of negotiation. The teacher, and only the teacher, is responsible for assigning grades for student performance.

Teachers need to establish clear expectations of student performance and to ensure that the process is not tainted in any way. Teachers need to be prepared to defend challenges to their grading system. They must also be fully aware of all district policies that relate to grading. Accumulating the minimum number of grades; assigning appropriate weight to homework, class work, projects, and tests; meeting deadlines; and informing students are all part of a process that must be beyond reproach.

To avoid controversy over grades, teachers can, for example, ask students to write down what grade they feel they honestly earned at the end of a marking period and to list any extenuating circumstances that occurred during that time, such as an illness, a death in the family, a family emergency, and so forth. By comparing the grade that students honestly feel they earned to the grade the teacher has calculated, the teacher has an opportunity to counsel students about their grades if there is a large discrepancy. This generally prevents upsetting students and parents when students get low grades. By being proactive, the teacher prevents nasty confrontations and controversy about grades.

SNAPSHOT 7-16

Invited Guest

Ms. Bowen, a young single parent who is about the same age as Mr. Dougherty, a teacher, is taking care of her younger brother, Robert, while his parents are on an extended vacation. Robert is in Mr. Dougherty's class, and after school one day, Ms. Bowen stops in to speak to him about Robert's progress. She also invites him to a family party the following Saturday. Mr. Dougherty accepts the invitation. When he arrives at the party, he notices a keg of beer on the porch and students from the school helping themselves.

Main Topic

Teacher as public persona

Subtopics

Extension of school authority

Substance abuse

Parental reaction

Possible Solutions

Mr. Dougherty should

1. Leave the party immediately, faking an illness.

2. Report the party to the police as soon as possible.

3. Sit in an area in which he cannot see the keg, so he can honestly say he never saw students drinking.

4. Be cool with the students, and drink up—he is not on school time or school property.

What Would You Do?

_____

_____

_____

_____

_____

What Really Happened

Mr. Dougherty left the party immediately and reported the incident to the administration, calling the principal at home. A neighbor of Ms. Bowen called the superintendent, an hour after Mr. Dougherty talked to the principal, to inform him that a member of the faculty had been at a party at which alcoholic beverages had been served to students. The superintendent submitted a report to the police, who, in turn, investigated the situation. Ms. Bowen was found guilty in municipal court of serving alcohol to minors; she was fined $500 and sentenced to 200 hours of community service.

What Should Have Happened and Why

Under similar circumstances, teachers must leave the party immediately and report the incident to an administrator in writing, documenting time and place.

Mr. Dougherty did a great job in recognizing this and the district's vulnerability in this situation. He took the appropriate actions, being proactive to protect himself and the school district.

"How Do You Like Yours?"

Mrs. Helman is an English teacher in the local high school. She and her family are walking through the local mall. One of her students, Ahmal, begins to shout loudly for all to hear that she likes to perform unnatural sex acts.

Main Topic

Teacher as public persona

Subtopics

Extension of school authority

Authority of teachers and the school

Possible Solutions

Mrs. Helman should

1. Contact mall security, and request that Ahmal be arrested.

2. Allow her husband to go after Ahmal to *teach him a lesson.*

3. Ignore the comments, because most people there do not know to whom Ahmal is referring.

4. Report the incident to school authorities the next school day.

What Would You Do?

_____

_____

_____

_____

_____

What Really Happened

Mrs. Helman reported the incident to the principal the next morning. Ahmal was suspended, because no other connection between him and the teacher existed outside the school. No appeal was made.

What Should Have Happened and Why

Teachers do not give up their protection from students just because they are outside the school building or are not on school time. However, the teacher must be prepared to report the incident in writing to the administration and be willing to testify if a court appearance is necessary.

Teachers are entitled to a reasonable expectation of privacy and the freedom to act as private citizens. Although teachers may be expected to live by higher standards within the community, they also have the right to expect the school district and the authorities to support them and prevent students from harassing them or members of their family. Effective teachers are willing to assert their rights in this arena for their own sakes as well as for the sakes of other teachers.

Reference

Wong, H. (speaker & author). (1990). *How you can be a super successful teacher* [Cassette recording]. Sunnyvale, CA: Harry K. Wong Tapes.

Afterword

As an astute reader, you have probably noticed that the issues presented in this book do not always relate to the curriculum in the school, methodologies used in teaching, or the daily classroom experiences of new teachers. The issues that cause the discussions in this book are generally social in nature.

Schools cannot educate students who are not ready to learn. Students who are involved in distracting social issues will not reach their potential as serious students. The social issues of substance abuse, child abuse, politics, union dominance, sexual behavior, safety, cheating, dress codes, rumors, misbehavior, tort liability, weapons, and violence have become the tails that wag the dog. All teachers must recognize that they will have an uphill battle unless these social issues are removed from their school and their individual classrooms. Every step taken in this direction, no matter how small, is critical to the survival of public education.

There is no magic formula that anyone can give to teachers to prevent these issues from crashing through the classroom door. Only through the best anticipation and preparation will teachers succeed. To each and every one of you who use this book as part of your preparation, I hope that it has given you some insight, wisdom, and common sense to help you build your teaching career on a firm foundation.

Good luck, and remember, you have the awesome responsibility and honor of influencing the most precious resource in our society—the children.

Bibliography

Canter, L., & Schadlow, B. (1990). *Lee Canter's parent conference book.* Santa Monica, CA: Lee Canter & Associates.

Crawford, D., & Bodine, R. (1996). *Conflict resolution education: A guide to programs in schools, youth-serving organizations, and community and juvenile justice settings.* Washington, DC: U.S. Department of Education.

Cummins, K. (1988). *The teacher's guide to behavioral interventions: Intervention strategies for behavior problems in the educational environment.* Columbia, MS: Hawthorne Educational Services.

Gardner, H. (1993). *Multiple intelligences: The theory in practice.* New York: Basic Books.

Ginott, H. (1972). *Teacher and child* (p. 15). New York: Macmillan.

Huston, T. C. (1993) Handling sexual harassment complaints. *NASB Employee Relations Quarterly, 1*(2), 6.

Jones, F., & Others (Eds.). (1987). *Strategic teaching and learning: Cognitive instruction in the content areas.* Alexandria, VA: Association for Supervision and Curriculum Development.

Karlin, M., & Berger, R. (1992). *Discipline and the disruptive child.* Englewood Cliffs, NJ: Parker.

Kohn, A. (1996). *Beyond discipline: From compliance to community.* Alexandria, VA: Association for Supervision and Curriculum Development.

Markova, D. (1992). *How your child is smart.* Berkeley, CA: Conari.

Maslow, A. H. (1970). *Motivation and personality.* New York: Harper & Row.

National School Board Association. (1993). *Violence in the schools: How America's school boards are safeguarding our children.* Alexandria, VA: Author.

Orange, C. (2000). *25 Biggest mistakes teachers make and how to avoid them.* Thousand Oaks, CA: Corwin.

Reif, S. (1993). *How to reach and teach ADD/ADHD children.* West Nyack, NY: The Center for Applied Research in Education.

Skinner, B. F. (1953). *Science and human behavior.* New York: Macmillan.

Underwood, M., & Dunne-Maxim, K. (1997). *Managing sudden traumatic loss in the schools.* Piscataway, NJ: University of Medicine and Dentistry of New Jersey.

United States Department of Education. (1999). *Taking responsibility for ending social promotion.* Washington, DC: U.S. Government Printing Office.

CORWIN
PRESS

The Corwin Press logo—a raven striding across an open book—represents the happy union of courage and learning. We are a professional-level publisher of books and journals for K–12 educators, and we are committed to creating and providing resources that embody these qualities. Corwin's motto is "Success for All Learners."